MULLIGAN'S WAKE

DAVE MULLIGAN

THE ISHMAEL TREE
NEW YORK   SHARJAH

Dave Mullgan/The Ishmael Tree
244 Fifth Avenue, 2nd Floor
New York, New York 10001
www.ishmaeltree.com
rightsandpermissions@ishmaeltree.com

Cover Art designed by: Charles Nemitz

Mulligan's Wake/ Dave Mulligan-- 1st ed.
ISBN 978-1-945959-23-3

Dedication

For my dad, who left long before I lived up to my potential. And to my living, loving family who've all seen me as I still struggle to do so. I love you.

And thanks for your patience.

Acknowledgements

Special thanks to: Mom (Trenna), James, Sara, Max, Mike, Leslie, Kathy, Brent, Andrew, Gigi and my crazy-hot, never boring, always laughing, Wendy.

What a ride it's been ... so far

PROLOGUE

I wore my father's tuxedo. I'm still not exactly sure why. The jacket was too tight in the shoulders because he was narrower than I am, so my arm movement was restricted. I thought about this in front of the bathroom mirror before emerging in it. As I looked at my reflection, I wondered briefly whether it was my dad's tux which was making me look older than my twenty-four years, but cobcluded that it was all of the crying, drinking, and sleepless nights over the past week which had aged me. I took my Ray Bans out of my shirt pocket, put them on, and turned my attention back to the snug-fitting dinner jacket. It didn't look quite as tight as it felt, and since I couldn't think of one possible scenario where I would be required to raise my arms above my head, I decided to go ahead and wear his tuxedo to his wake. Perhaps, technically, it wasn't a "wake" because his body was not there on display, as it is practiced in traditional Irish living rooms (I know. Ironic). This I never would have allowed. I'm not saying that the decision would have been mine to make, but if my mother or anybody else would have moved to lay my dad out for public scrutiny I would have complained so vehemently that it just never would have happened. Call me a dark cloud, but I can't think of a better way to ruin a party than to use a dead person for the center piece. What are "viewers" expected to say at those things?

"Yep. He's dead alright."

"It's almost ironic because he was always the life of the party."

"Boy, he looks like a million bucks..."

This is a moot issue anyway because my father had been cremated and his ashes were in a little cardboard box in the trunk of my mother's Mustang parked in front of the house. I've only disclosed this family secret to two or three people because I'm aware of how it sounds. Allow me to try and explain by saying that we were an extremely tight, happy, laughing family and that we were completely unaccustomed to, and unprepared for, death. My father was the center of our family. He was our leader, our teacher, and our biggest fan. He was above death. So when the unthinkable happened without even a whisper of warning, none of us took it upon ourselves to slip into the normal death-in-the-family routine and make the "arrangements." There was no funeral. A psychologist may analyze this behavior, this complete lack of compliance with proper death etiquette, and conclude that we did not accept his passing. But that was not the case. We accepted the fact that he was gone. So much so, in fact, that deciding upon the final resting place for his ashes was secondary to our consoling one another and adjusting as a family to a world without him. And our first step toward recovery was deciding to have a party for my father. A wake, without the body.

Of course, there were the expected relatives, friends, coworkers and neighbors in attendance. It was awkward at times, feigning fresh responses to repeated, well-meant comments such as "at least he went quickly," but I knew that it must have been even more awkward for these well-wishers so I tolerated it all. The guests that I appreciated the most and found most interesting were the ones whom I'd never seen before and those who had never been in our home.

I met a few of them. They'd read of my father's death in the newspaper and made the effort to come not out of any family obligation, but of pure admiration and affection for a man they'd come to know. Strangely, these people also made me the saddest. I'd just filled my beer at the keg out on the back deck over-looking a rolling golf course and the ocean beyond. This had always been my father's favorite view. He'd stand at the rail for long periods as the sun set, sipping a glass of red wine, admiring and appreciating what he'd been able to provide for his family. I was about to re-enter the party when an unfamiliar man of about forty joined me on the deck. I'd noticed him a little while earlier standing alone inside.

"Excuse me," he said nervously, "you're Mister Mulligan's son, aren't you?"

"Yes, I'm Dave."

"I'm pleased to meet you, Dave. I'm Ron. You don't know me." He was obviously uncomfortable as we shook hands.

"It's nice to meet you Ron."

"I just came because I was so sorry to hear about your father."

"Thank you. How did you know my dad?"

"Well, I really didn't know him very well. I just saw him once a week or so. I work at Baskin Robbins up at Peninsula Center. He'd stop in on his way home from work to get an ice cream cone, chocolate and vanilla, and he was always so funny and just such a nice man. When you work in a place like that, not all your customers are that way. I know that he worked in TV, and that he made a lot of money, but he always treated me like I was just as important as he was. Like we were friends. I'll always remember him for that, and I just wanted to come here and tell someone in his family that he was my friend."

Ron left immediately after talking to me. I stayed out on the deck and thought about what he'd said about my father. I thought about him stopping in alone to get an ice cream cone on his way home from work. Chocolate and vanilla. Something a boy would do. I never knew that he did that. I wondered what kinds of other little things he did which I'd never know about. I was grateful to Ron for telling me, because he'd also made me realize that I was being selfish with my grief. I'd been clinging to it like I was the only one who was really hurting, but there were so many others, including people whom I'd never know, who were experiencing their own private sadness. It wasn't just mine. He wasn't just mine.

He'd belonged to all of us, and he was gone. I looked out over the ocean and cried again. You can tell a lot about a man by looking at the people who gather after his death. A good mingler could have gotten an excellent impression of exactly what sort of man my father was. There were representatives present from every facet of his life. I have a theory that if you compile all of the character attributes and personality traits of every person who attends a man's post-death gathering and then simply blend them all together, you'll have a perfect composite character description of the deceased.

One of my father's dearest friends, political satirist / humorist Mark Russell, began his eulogy by noting that Jim Mulligan had died just as he had lived — neatly. This was true. My father had always been neat. Not in a prissy sort of way, yet, oddly, for a creative, fun-loving person, he was simply happier when things around him were tidy. His physical appearance was equally well-kept. He carried no fat, no extra baggage, on his small, light frame. His Irish hair was like coiled copper wire, and had the potential for that wild Einstein look, but he spent several minutes every morning patting it down against his head. He kept his red/grey beard short and tight, clipping it almost daily. No clutter in his life. No messes. And sure enough, one day while watching the World Series on TV, he had quietly nodded off, just as if he were taking a brief nap, and slipped neatly away. He was 55.

After the eulogy, a tall man I'd never seen before asked for the crowd's attention and made his way up to the front of perhaps two-hundred weeping souls.

Murmuring swept through the mourners; it seemed that nobody knew him. When he achieved the front and center position, I saw that he carried a violin case. He placed the case on the coffee table next to him, opened it, and first produced the bow. He then lifted out a hand saw; the sort which hangs and slowly gathers rust on the garage wall of most American families.

My first thought was that he was some sort of sick, frustrated, out-of-work magician who had crashed the wake in order to perform his tricks for a defenseless crowd weakened by mourning. He then began to speak. He introduced himself as Jack and claimed that he knew my father from the tennis club. My father was, indeed, a member of the club just down the road, and was, in fact, the possessor of what was perhaps the poorest, stiffest serve in the history of the sport. When Jack alluded briefly to the total lack of fluidity in my father's tennis game, I knew that he was no imposter and he'd earned my attention.

"I saw Jim Mulligan two or three times a month down at the club. He really loved to play, but he worked so much that he couldn't play often enough to get as good as he wanted to be, so he'd get frustrated with himself. We were sitting together in the clubhouse having a beer one evening after losing a doubles match to a couple of doctors, and I mentioned to Jim that I could play the saw. 'Play the saw?' he asked, like I was crazy. I told him that, yeah, I could play the saw. I explained that I used a bow like a violinist uses, and that I

→

can make music with an ordinary hand saw. He thought I was kidding at first, but when I told him that I was serious, he said that I was delusional and that I should just stay indoors (a few nervous chuckles interrupt the otherwise silent room). After that it became sort of a running joke with us. Every time I'd see him I'd promise that I'd play the saw for him some time, and he'd make some wise-crack about me needing therapy or something (more chuckles). I put my saw and bow in the back of my car a couple of weeks ago so I could play it for him the next time I saw him. And then I read about Jim's death in the paper. (Jack's voice wavered and he nearly began to cry, but then regained his composure and proceeded.) So, Jim, wherever you are (Jack, of course, had no idea that my father was parked right out front in the trunk of my mother's Mustang), this tune is for you..."

He lifted the saw to his chin in as dignified a manner as the most seasoned concert violinist would raise his Stradivarius. With the wooden handle beneath his chin and lying flat on his shoulder, he held the end of the blade at arm's length with his fingertips. He then shifted his shoulder, cocked his chin and slowly raised the bow. Many in the crowd stirred nervously, clearly unsure of how to digest this unorthodox interruption. Some were so put off that they began filtering out of the room in disgust. I looked over at my mother, still teary-eyed from Mark Russell's eulogy, and she shrugged in passive acquiescence. Then Jack began to play the saw.

The tune he'd chosen was "Danny Boy," perhaps the saddest and most heart-wrenching melody ever composed. Yet, when played on the saw, it was even more so. As he drew the bow across the broad side of the blade, he simultaneously bowed and manipulated the metal with pressure from his fingertips, creating a haunting whine, as though the steel were weeping.

It was a rare moment in time when sound, circumstance and emotion fell together in perfect sync, and many in the room, I for one, drifted away to a time and place where my father still lived.

It was when the song had ended and my mind had drifted back to the party that I realized how funny the situation was and how perfectly it punctuated the end of my father's life. He'd been gone for a week and this total stranger had just appeared and played Danny Boy on a hand saw in our living room. I was suddenly overwhelmed by how perfect it was; how fitting a tribute to a man who had always managed to keep his family laughing and had made his living by his sense of humor. I cheered aloud and shot my arms skyward in delight and split the back of my father's tuxedo.

I closed the bathroom door, locked it, and faced the mirror again, this time to assess the damage I'd just done to my dad's tuxedo. I first attempted to check the damage to the jacket while still wearing it. I turned my back to the mirror and strained to look over my shoulder, then heard another rip. "Fuck."

I took the jacket off in disgust, took a quick look at the eight-inch tear, and flung it on the counter next to the sink. My dad had owned the tuxedo for over ten years and it had still looked new. I'd worn it for three hours and shredded it. I looked at my reflection and I shook my head, just as my father would have done upon discovering what I'd just done.

Then I moved closer to the mirror and removed my sunglasses. This was the first time I'd had real eye contact with myself since my father's death; the first time I'd had the courage to see what I looked like without my father in the world. I leaned closer. My eyes were bloodshot and horribly swollen, and the pain had left new lines, yet, I could see that, beneath this mask of sorrow and insecurity, I still resided.

I became locked in a stare with myself. Reality was crashing down around me. The man I'd most wanted to impress in the world was gone before I'd had the chance to show him what I could do. He'd always felt that I was wasting great potential, and he'd had me believing him, yet

I'd been waiting for just the right time to begin my assault on the world. I'd waited too long. And now, as I looked at myself, into myself, questions began to form. Would the death of my father be the impetus I required to get me to grow up? If so, then how ironic. Or, because my biggest fan was no longer out there in the audience, would I lose the motivation to perform entirely? It was at that moment, as I stood face to face with my own reflection during my father's wake, that I first began to ponder leaving the country and embarking on a great adventure to find out what kind of man I was without my father.

When the bittersweet celebration was coming to a close, a man who had worked with my father was saying good-bye to my family at the front door. He hugged my mother and my sister, shook my brother's hand, and then mine. As he turned to leave, he said "Hell of a wake."

I almost said something about it not really being a wake, but then it struck me that the word might be appropriate after all. The world was a different place without him, and the umbilical cord which had always bound us had been prematurely severed, yet, because of the love he'd instilled in me and in the family, I knew that no matter what happened I would spend the rest of my life living in my father's wake.

The Decision

To this day I haven't decided whether it was an act of cowardice or one of bravery. Perhaps I'll be an old man before I know; I'll be terrorizing my neighborhood in a sporty electric wheelchair when suddenly I'll hit the brakes and nod to myself with a look of peaceful self-discovery behind my trifocals. Or maybe I'll never decide. What's done is done, though, and I won't change my history with a judgement in hindsight. My older friends, those of the same generation as my parents, told me that I was running away from reality.

"You've been drifting since your dad died and now you're just running away." Certainly, a brave man does not "run away;" therefore it may be noted that the older crowd viewed my trip as an act of cowardice.

The sub-fifties took a different view. When I explained to any of my contemporaries that I had basically sold my life and bought a plane ticket to Australia, the reaction was just as predictable as that of the elders — but opposite. A childish smile would claim the lips, then the eyes would roll slightly up and off-center into a daydream angle, indicating that the mind had drifted across the Pacific to an Australia that they could only imagine - and visions of kangaroos hopped in their heads. "God, I've always wanted to do that, but I've never had the nerve to just quit my job and go." It may be noted that my contemporary friends viewed my dropping everything to go to Australia as an act of bravery.

The vast distance between the poles of opinion fascinated me. Did my elders, in their hard-earned wisdom, see something, know something, that those sharing my generation and I were overlooking? Could it be true that I was about to waste an entire year of my life? Or were those of the twenty-five to thirty group rectified in their "go for it" concurrence? I toyed with the idea that maybe my elders had forgotten something, had shed a part of themselves as they drifted into middle age which left them incapable of understanding such a drastic deviation from the norm. I didn't really believe this theory, but in my insecure state I clung to it because I had already made up my mind that I was going to Australia.

I don't wish to appear as though I paid no attention to the words of wisdom offered me by my elders. I did listen. We held many long discussions in which I was forced to defend my decision to leave.

"I'm going to learn as I travel and add to my reservoir of knowledge."

"I'm going to learn how to rough it and learn the true value of the dollar."

"I'm going to find myself."

"I've always been curious as to what Australians eat" (some of my points were stronger than others).

"I'm going to see things and be inspired to write a great book along the way. Or a movie.

Or a play..."

At those desperate moments when I struggled and reached for plausible reasons for my leaving, I realized that I was trying to convince myself as much as I was trying to convince them that what I was about to do was the right thing. I wrestled with it constantly, finally coming to the conclusion that the answer would be determined by what I accomplished during my adventure. To better understand why I would quit my job, sell my car — basically drop everything - and buy a plane ticket to Australia, you should have some idea of the state of my life at the time.

Nothing had changed since my father's death. Career-wise, I had none. I had a job, but a job is all it was. I've been told countless times in my life that I am a "natural born salesman," (this defamatory title always brought to mind the image of a prickish five-year-old in a polyester suit, running a lemonade stand. "Step right up, friends, and spend the smartest five cents of your life").

Coming as no great surprise to anybody, I filled the niche expected of me and I became a salesman. My first sales job was in automobiles. Yes, I was a "car salesman." The car salesman is universally held in low regard and is generally considered to be one of nature's most primitive creatures. You'll hear no argument from me on this; if all the world's people were placed inside a giant barrel, shaken up, and allowed to settle, there would be a thin residue of car salesmen at the very bottom, just below the axe murderers and televangelists.

I learned very quickly in the car business that the bigger one's heart, the smaller one's paycheck. Not uncommon was the situation where I would find myself across the desk from a sweet, struggling, young couple who trusted me and would have paid any amount that I asked of them. I would look at them and know that they were buying the car out of utter necessity, perhaps to accommodate their first child, still in the young mother's womb. It's a tough position to be in if you are the possessor of even a small conscience.

But the typical car salesman has long since forgotten the concept of "conscience," and would almost certainly be sporting a sales boner under the desk in this situation. After guiding the young couple to a commitment on a dollar figure, the smiling salesman would then excuse himself from their presence so that he may attain final approval on the deal from God, located behind the black door at the end of the hall.

This is where the "sales manager" resides. This is his den. He has probably been watching the entire slaughter through one of those one-way mirrors, like the ones in detectives' interrogation rooms and that fraternities have in their ladies' bathrooms, and he's excited. The kind salesman would soon re-emerge with the day-saving news that his boss only wanted twelve-hundred dollars more than the agreed-upon figure. He would then shake the hands of the naive, young couple, congratulate them on a deal that actually cost them four thousand dollars too much, and ask them if they had entertained any thoughts of trading the baby in after its birth.

Selling cars, I decided, was not for me. I understand perfectly that, for any business to thrive, there must be a margin of profit. That's fundamental. But, somewhere along the line, the automobile business was infiltrated by sleazy bastards and has fallen into a darkened state of disrepair. It's a dimly-lit alley through which we all must pass at some point, and we do it with caution and mistrust. The profit is often achieved through deceit, and the size thereof is directly proportionate to the customer's naivete.

Not only did I find myself unable to do business dishonestly, I also found myself incapable of doing business with attractive women. When it came to dealing with a pretty lady, I was never accused of mixing business with pleasure; as soon as I saw her walk onto the car lot, I forgot about business entirely. I didn't care whether she was there to buy a car or to paint one, I just wanted to meet her and be close to her. I'm perfectly aware that this sounds despicable, but I truly didn't think so while it was happening.

Soon after fleeing the dark world of the car business, I found myself in another sales position. Roofs. I sold roofs. Now, when it begins to rain in ones living room and one decides that it is time to get a new roof, one does not go to the "roof store" and pick one out. He or she would call a roofing company for some professional advice and an estimate.

Soon thereafter, I, being a roofing salesman, would arrive at the door armed with a big smile and a big tape measure. I would then assemble my sectional ladder (which occupied the passenger seat of my 1961 Austin Healey), climb up onto the roof, take the necessary measurements, climb down again, and explain to Mrs. Home-alone exactly how much it was going to cost to keep the inside part of her home dry this winter. If I were charming enough and professional enough, she would sign the contract on the spot. Most, however, would wait to discuss it with the "man of the house."

Although the money was pretty good in roofs and I was basically my own boss, I viewed it as just another job and certainly did not see myself making a career in shingles. I was coasting along and making enough money to pay my rent and support my sins, but I lacked the motivation necessary to stand out among the rest of the roofing salesmen and make myself a lot of money. I settled for being "average" because it was easy and comfortable and didn't require much effort.

When I had escaped the car business months before, I had carried with me the crippling disorder which rendered me useless as a salesman when doing business with an attractive woman. And this problem became immeasurably more complex due to the simple fact that the majority of my business as a roofing salesman was carried out with bored housewives in the home behind closed doors. More than one deal was consummated in the master bedroom, although, by that time, I had almost certainly forgotten the original purpose of my visit.

My obsession with attractive women needs further excavation. Allow me to begin by saying that it wasn't something of which I was proud. Just as I do now, I viewed it, even then, as an affliction. A rather enjoyable affliction, but an affliction nonetheless and one which was seriously hindering my growth. Looking back, I liken myself to one of those annoying, little, shiny-eyed, panting dogs that spends all waking hours in search of something to mount.

I developed a reputation in the community as a "womanizer," and it became increasingly difficult for me to find a girl who would take me seriously. There are few things as ego-bruising to a male as being laughed at heartily by a girl whom he's just asked out for a date. It happened to me many times; whenever my reputation arrived someplace before I did. In my deluded, hyper-hormonal state, however, I felt that I was being misunderstood and I tried to convey this feeling numerous times....

".. no, no, you've got me all wrong. Sure, I go out with a few girls, but what's wrong with that? I like these girls. They're my friends."

SHE: "Do you have sex with these 'friends' of yours?"

ME: "Why are you asking me that?"

SHE: "Because I refuse to be just another girl on your list."

ME: "List? I don't keep a list. If and when I'm intimate with a girl, I do it because it's beautiful and it's fun and we both want to do it. You think you've got me all figured out, don't you?"

SHE: "How many girls have you been to bed with?"

ME: "I have no idea, I don't count. Any guy who keeps track of how many girls he's slept with is an asshole."

SHE: "Fifty?"

ME: "Way more than that..."

SHE: "I'd never go out with you."

ME: "But you don't understand ... I like you"

SHE: "I like you too, but I don't like what you are."

ME: "What am I?"

SHE: "You're a womanizer."

ME: "What is your definition of a womanizer?"

SHE: "A womanizer is a guy who goes around picking up girls and sleeping with as many as he can."

ME: "Does this feel as though I'm trying to pick you up? We're just sitting here having a nice conversation."

SHE: "A good womanizer never makes a girl feel as though she's being picked up."

ME: "Well, I don't feel I have to sit here and be subjected to all of this criticism. I'm going home. Would you like to come with me?"

A young man who finds happiness only in the pursuit and conquest of pretty girls would have enough trouble making anything of himself, yet I possessed another even more serious flaw which was hindering my progress. The condition has many names, depending upon who's doing the name-calling. My mother referred to me lovingly as a "ne'er-do-well"; my sister as her "crazy brother"; and many of the stiffer citizens in the community referred to me as *That Wild Mulligan*. These terms are sugar-coated euphemisms for what can only truly be described as an asshole.

Yes, I was an asshole. I was not, however, the sort of asshole who would steal your wallet or insult your grandmother. No, nothing that malicious. I was the type of asshole who would sneak into your backyard and shave your prize poodle just to see how funny he'd look with no hair. I would usually be arrested two or three times a year for such assholosities; certainly pardonable for a young man of sixteen or seventeen. But these periodic arrests continued well into my twenties. One night, just two weeks before I stepped onto the airplane to fly to Australia, I found myself running away from a determined policeman at the age of twenty-six. The wings of fear flap mighty fast and I was able to escape my pursuer-in-blue, but reality travels at the speed of light and I couldn't out run the fact that I was still an asshole. I had always assumed that this, among the worst of my afflictions, would dilute with age, but it was showing no indication of doing so and this scared me.

I'll give you a perfect example of vintage asshole. I was twenty-five and my father had only been dead for a year when it happened. Actually, to say "when it happened" is misleading because that makes it sound as though I was a victim of external forces. I wasn't. The idea was conceived and nurtured in my head and I accept full responsibility. I was twenty-five when I did it.

It was early January, and the batteries included with most holiday gifts were beginning to run low. Most of the Christmas trees had been stripped of their ornaments and hauled out to curbside for the trash man (an act with which I've never been comfortable. Surely there must be a more respectful, ceremonious way to dispose of what has been the very focal point of Christmas.

What a display of insensitivity. Next we'll be doing the same thing with our elderly, "Boy, it's a lucky thing ol' Grandpa kicked off on trash day, huh? If the ol' fart had lasted another day, we'd a had to keep him in the garage till they come again on Tuesday").

On a cold Friday night (well, cold by Southern California standards), I was invited to a very special dinner party at a friend's house. It was a "Dave Dinner." The host and all four guests were named Dave. We had all grown up in the same large circle of friends and often laughed about our parents' lack of imagination in giving us the generic moniker. One of the Daves decided to make the best of it and it was his idea to hold the exclusive dinner party. There were other friends who wanted to attend, but they had such names as Buck, Pete and Griff, so they couldn't come. It was to be a rather formal occasion, so we all donned our ties and jackets and made a pretty sharp-looking pack of Daves.

Dave's mom prepared an incredible four-course meal and I cannot recall a single moment at the table when one of us was not laughing. "Pass the gravy, would you Dave?" Cheap laughs were piling high. I was even wearing an old name tag I had acquired somewhere years before on a short-lived job. It was plain and white and simply read "Dave."

After dinner, we headed as a group to our old faithful watering hole, Hennessey's Tavern, for a few beers. I'm certain that half the reason we went there was so that we could approach people and say "Hi, we're Dave" (which we continued to do long after it had lost all of its humor to those in the bar). We were on a roll. We were thinking as one. We were Dave.

When last call was sounded at Hennessey's, we all agreed that the time for our collective fun to end had not yet arrived. I proclaimed and all agreed that we would sneak into Marineland of the Pacific, just ten minutes down the coastal road (Marineland, which is no longer there, was like a slightly smaller version of Seaworld). This was something we'd all done more than twice while growing up, and this seemed like a perfect opportunity to reach back and grab a handful of the good ol' days.

Thirty minutes later, we giggled like kids as we climbed the fence surrounding the aquapark, still in our ties, and jumped down onto the dew-damp grass at two-thirty in the morning. Our objective was to sneak past any unsuspecting security guards to the killer whale tank located in the center of the park. The plan was to then creep down onto the small floating platform and pet the two black & white giants.

There's something indescribably exciting about sneaking into a place where you're not allowed. Slithering past an armed security guard really gets the heart going. I'm not sure what the other Daves were thinking, but I was fantasizing that I was on a vital, top secret mission and the future of world peace was in my hands. Then I looked down and saw that I had gotten mud all over my tie and the moment was spoiled.

It took us nearly an hour to get past security and to our objective. The killer whale tank was designed like a miniature stadium, with ascending concentric rows of seats surrounding the water and providing capacity for several hundred spectators. A single lightbulb hung high above the center of the tank, faintly illuminating the stadium and making the water look as black as oil.

The tank itself was a perfect cylinder, with a diameter of about sixty feet, and a depth of roughly eighty. I had probably seen the killer whales close to a hundred times since I was a young boy, but the feeling of awe upon entering the arena never waned as I grew older. It was not merely their great size which impressed me, it was also the keen awareness which they exuded; not merely the awareness of my physical presence, but awareness of what I was, and maybe even who I was.

Orky and Corky (dorky names certainly beneath such noble animals) appeared to be sleeping as the five of us slipped down the ladder, one by one, onto the small floating platform where the trainers would normally stand while conducting shows. We each kneeled, silently facing the water, and waited for them. The Orcas slept on the surface, side by side, directly across the tank from the platform. Their lack of any sort of reaction indicated that they had not yet sensed our presence.

I remembered a trick I had learned as a kid, and I slipped my hand into the chilly water and snapped my fingers. Instantly, the pair of sleeping giants submerged and disappeared into the black water. We glanced at one another and peered nervously into the depths, waiting. Five long seconds later, they appeared just a foot in front of us, mouths wide open, exhibiting huge, white, conical teeth. We jumped up and back, did a 180-degree spin and said, "oh fuck," all in a unison the Pips would have admired.

Three of the Daves scrambled up the ladder without touching a rung, leaving two of us standing timidly on the platform. The whales, it became apparent, were not flashing their choppers as a threat, but, instead, they had surfaced open-mouthed expecting a mackerel or two to be lobbed their way as part of their normal training routine. And there we stood ... fishless. We had nothing to offer the whales but our company. The other three Daves succumbed to the momentum of their fear and fled into the night. Four mammals remained; two of which being highly intelligent.

I was finding it extremely difficult to walk away from the whales. It was probably my imagination, but I felt a bond with them, plus that old feeling that they knew me was coming back. The warm feeling swelled inside of me and left no room for fear. Without saying a word to Dave, I stepped off of the platform and onto Corky's back. I sat down just behind the blowhole, and she began to move away from the platform like a submarine leaving its berth.

As we began to make our way around the tank, I looked back over my shoulder at Dave, still standing on the platform. He looked at me, then down at Orky, the big male parked at curbside, and then back at me. I waved to show him that I was alright, and, a second later, he was seated on Orky, the other killer whale.

And, so began thirty minutes of raw, unfiltered joy. As our confidence grew, we began to relax and ham it up a little. We stood on their backs and surfed, clockwise, around and around the tank. My loafers were waterlogged and my knit tie drooped below my waist, but my adrenaline soared and it was euphoric. I carry a fond image of a moment when Dave and I were seated on our respective whales, legs crossed, leaning back against the dorsal fin as though on giant floating lounge chairs as they continued their casual laps around the tank. The Orcas had separated and Dave and I circled the tank directly across from one another.

"I wonder what the other Daves are doing?" I said aloud.

"Who cares?" Dave answered, grinning.

All good whale rides must come to an end, and ours ended abruptly. Having heard our laughter, a disbelieving security guard stormed into the arena waving his gun and the fun was over. The rest of the morning was dominated by hostile men in uniform, and ended on the cold steel of a county jail cell.

"What are ya' in for?" a tattooed, felon-sort asked me.

"Trespassing," I told him.

I must admit that there was one moment during my legal processing when I felt complete humiliation. It was the following afternoon when I was being released from custody. The officer on duty returned to me the possessions which I carried on my person at the time of our incarceration. In an envelope was my belt, a water-soaked knit tie and a plastic nametag which read "DAVE."

The media ate up the story of the midnight whale ride, and we made national news for the next week. I wasn't ashamed of what I had done, it was harmless, but it was embarrassingly typical of a pattern which had been developing for years. The incident fit so perfectly into the "Big Picture" of my life that it seemed as though the space had been reserved for it. And I had almost certainly clinched an eternal seat in the Southern California Asshole Hall of Fame.

I believe that our memories and accomplishments, our goals and ambitions, our outlooks and our attitudes, all come together into a unique formula — and that it who we are. I felt that there was something terribly wrong with my formula, and it just wasn't adding up right. I wasn't accomplishing anything because my goals and ambitions were ambiguous and un-defined. My life's plan rarely extended beyond the coming Saturday night, and this aimlessness led to my pursuing the peripheral distractions. This extreme short-sightedness, however, was not merely confined to the way I saw my fu-ture; it was also how I saw, or didn't see, the world itself out-side of my little opaque bubble of fun.

Had I not been born into a world where somebody had already invented clocks and calendars, I would have had ab-solutely no concept of time. I would have never observed a pattern in the sun's daily appearance. Had I not been told otherwise, I would have assumed that the Earth was flat. I never would have thought of wearing clothes or building a shelter to escape the rain; perhaps I would have gone so far as to stand under a tree, but I doubt it. I would have probably crouched naked on the ground and wondered to myself whether or not the rain would ever stop falling on me. The point of all this is that I felt as though the only reason I had achieved any level of civility was due to the fact that I was born into pre-existing civilization.

All of the accomplishments of humanity, all of the symbols of progress and the luxuries and amenities of modern times were achieved by others and handed to me at birth because I just happened to be born in the year 1962. I was twenty-six years old and I realized that I was still just a boy and I didn't have a clue. My womanizing, excessive drinking and being an asshole were not the problems. They were the symptoms.

My solution? Get away. I'd been considering it for the two years since my father's death, and it suddenly seemed like the time was right. I wanted to get a long look at myself and my life from a distance and see then if I could isolate the problems and make the necessary changes.

Leaving the country was to be my way of backing off to put things in focus. I chose Australia for two reasons; because I'd heard that it was still raw, wild, and unspoiled, making it perfect ground for adventure; and because they spoke English there and I wouldn't have to learn another language.

On a Monday afternoon in early November, 1988, I picked up the yellow pages and opened to "Travel." My travel agent, a pretty Australian girl, disclosed to me the fact that, for only two hundred dollars additional to the round-trip ticket to Australia, I could also fly to New Zealand, The Cook Islands, Fiji, and Hawaii. I thought it over for a moment and said,

"Okay, I'll go there too." The only set date for the entire journey was the day of departure from Los Angeles. The rest of the flight dates were left open. The only real limitation was that I had to complete the entire flight circuit within one year. I paid for my ticket and set my departure date: November 28th. This was just two days after Thanksgiving. My family wanted me to wait until after Christmas, but I felt that I wouldn't be able to make it that long. I was sure I'd tumble and self-destruct by mid-December.

With my big decision made, I began to feel stronger than I could ever remember feeling. I see now that this was due to the fact that I had just made the first major decision for myself in my entire life. All others previously had been made for me because I lacked the foresight and decisiveness to make them myself. This may or may not have been the right decision, but it was mine and it was a move. I had ceased to merely drift along with the current; I was swimming ahead on my own into unfamiliar waters.

With my date of departure approaching quickly, it was soon time for me to prepare. This was actually the easy part. I quit my job selling roofs, sold my car and had a party. And a grand party it was, with all of my closest friends, new and old, there to say good-bye and wish me luck.

I noticed that many of them, mostly the girls, were worried that I would pull some asshole maneuver along the way and get myself hurt or killed. "Just be careful," I heard over and over. I assured them that I would and that the next time they saw me, I would be a man. I actually said (after many farewell beers), "There's a man out there somewhere by the name of Dave Mulligan, and I'm going to find him and bring him back."

The big day, November the 28th, 1988, arrived, and I still hadn't purchased any of my supplies for the trip. I went to an outdoorsy-type store and bought a backpack and a sleeping bag. I figured I'd need some extra socks and underwear, so I bought some of those too, along with toiletries (a favorite word of mine). And, so I was equipped. Packing consisted of stuffing as many articles of clothing into my new backpack as I could. One backpack, one year. I liked the concept.

I kept the last, most intimate good-byes short and to the point. That was unlike me, for I possess a weakness in my character which usually causes me to allow a farewell to continue far too long and, therefore, lose its potency. I kept it to ten minutes with Sabrina, a significant female figure in my life at the time, and I was quite proud of myself. I desperately fought the urges to hug and kiss her and grovel at her feet, but I was strong and kept my chin up (and if you had a look at Sabrina, an absolute vision of Asian persuasion, you'd know what I mean. In fact, if I had that good-bye to say again, I'd grovel).

My brother and sister drove me to the airport where I checked in and handed over my backpack. The three of us then moved promptly to the bar. I've always loved my brother and sister far beyond the mechanical family obligation that so many siblings feel for one another. They are among my very favorite people and the fact that they happened to be born as my brother and sister was my great fortune. As the three of us toasted to what the coming year might bring, Emily showed up.

Emily, a lovely, wholesome, Mid-western girl, was about as close to being my girlfriend as anybody could have been at that time. She remains a true rarity whose disarming physical beauty is matched by a heart and character of equal appeal. If I had been man enough, I would have stayed and done my best to make her my one-and-only, but I was still just a boy with nothing to offer her and it was time for me to leave.

I was scared sitting there in the airport. Everything was happening so fast. The strength which I had found in making the Big Decision was waning a bit and I was experiencing the strange sensation that I was no longer leaving, but being taken. I attributed the feeling to cold feet and did my best to suppress it.

At 8:25 p.m., I said good-bye to three whom I loved, then turned and jogged through the terminal toward Australia and the South Pacific and, hopefully, my manhood.

TWO

The Magic Chamber

I've always maintained a love/hate relationship with flying. Part of me appreciates flying for the incredible technology and the raw power of the big jets, while the other part of me is scared shitless.

Turbulence and banking turns stop my breath because I'm reminded that I'm miles above the earth in a metal tube traveling at many hundreds of miles per hour. I've sat breathless and white-knuckled while flying and constructed detailed theories on how technology should progress at a natural rate with evolution and that we as humans have reached too far beyond ourselves into the future and grasped the power of air travel prematurely.

Having absolutely no control over the situation causes me great discomfort. I feel that there should be a little toy steering wheel in front of every seat on a plane to pacify people like me during moments of terror. I've found alcohol to be the next best remedy and, therefore, can be counted on to indulge rather heavily before and during all flights which include my name on the passenger list. If I throw a few beers across my chest before stepping onto an airplane, it transforms the cabin into a kind of magic chamber. I'm in one city when they close the door behind me, and when they re-open it to let me out ... voilà! I'm somewhere new! It isn't that simple on a fourteen-hour flight (which is what the first leg of my trip was), but it does have a relaxing effect and makes it much easier to forget that I'm suspended in the sky.

As I was being whisked across the Pacific, I had plenty of time to contemplate the immensity of the step I had just taken. Since making the decision to leave one month before, the trip had merely been an abstract idea — something about which to boast down at Hennessey's over a few beers. But inside, deep down, I never truly believed that it would happen. I would either be arrested, or hit by a car, or Libya would decide to invade Australia and not allow any American visitors -- something would happen to prevent my actually leaving for a year. But nothing had happened.

The only possibility remaining which could have prevented me from making it down under would have been for the plane to fall into the sea. I quickly ordered another beer from a passing flight attendant and fell asleep in the magic chamber.

Although I was in the sky somewhere over the middle of the Pacific Ocean, streaking like a comet away from everybody I knew in the world, there was still one person I needed to convince that my trip was not going to be a wasted year. It had been two years since my dad had died, yet there was no one's approval I sought more than his. I didn't feel that he was "watching over me" or that he could hear me; I dealt with his death realistically. When my dad died, my dad died. I felt that "life after death" was a silly convenience invented by people unable to accept the harsh reality of mortality.

Yet, I had known him so well and loved him so much, that, as I lived on after his death and continued my slow development into manhood, my relationship with him continued to develop as well. As I made new discoveries about myself and about the world, I learned more about what he was and what he meant. And when I was faced with a new situation, I often based my decision on what I felt he would have done or advised me to do. This is not to say that I would have taken his advice, but I surely would have listened to it because he was always very logical and methodical. He certainly would have had quite a bit to say about my leaving and I had been avoiding a confrontation with him since I'd made the big decision. As I slept on the plane he caught up with me.

"You know, Dave, you're pissing your life away."

"I knew you'd think that. I'm not 'pissing my life away,' that's what I was doing at home.

This is going to be a growing experience for me."

"That's bullshit and you know it. Tell me what you think you're going to accomplish in Australia that you couldn't do at home."

"I'm going to learn how to be on my own... how to make it completely on my own..."

"You're twenty-six years old! Don't you think you should know how to make it on your own by now?"

"I know I should, but I don't. That's why I've left. I need to find out how. If I'm alone on the other side of the world, I won't have any choice, will I?"

"I've never understood you. I don't know, maybe it's my own fault. I just know I see a young man who's got the world by the balls, but you're afraid to squeeze. Your friends are just flying past you. This trip is just another easy way out for you. It's a vacation. A party. Life was getting a little tough, so you're running away. Just like you did with college. Don't you see the pattern? I'll tell you something, Dave. I'm scared for you. I'm really scared for you."

"I'll be alright. You know me. I always end up alright. I'll show you."

"I know you'll be alright. But alright is for the average. You're so much better than that."

"I'm hoping that, when this adventure is over, I'll be more like you."

"You always know the right thing to say."

"I love you dad."

"I love you too, son."

I re-awoke sometime later with my mouth wide open and a trail of drool leading across my cheek. This is an embarrassing condition, but is not frowned upon on airplanes because it happens to everybody once. I'm told that it even happens to those flying in first class (I've never witnessed this personally, but a friend of mine once snuck up into first class and saw with his own eyes a very important-looking man in a three-piece suit asleep with his head hanging over the aisle and a rope of drool swinging from his chin. My friend told me it made him feel good somehow).

I then began to notice that something had happened during those two hours that I was asleep. Everyone on the plane, even the crew, was suffering from the inevitable "Flight Face." Nobody can escape this condition. Some may be afflicted sooner than others, but everybody on the plane will have it after four or five hours. It's actually the hair that goes first. It begins to look as though you haven't washed it for a couple of days, and becomes very limp. The more you comb it, the flatter it gets. Soon thereafter, the skin loses all color and begins to take on a clay like dullness. New blemishes are born and bags form under the eyes. Morning breath quickly follows. I'm convinced that the airlines took flight face into consideration when they decided to arrange the seats so that they all face in one direction. They would have arranged them to accommodate a more social atmosphere, but imagine the discomfort we'd all feel if we had to sit and gawk at one another in that horrid condition. Think of the flight attendants who must maintain some level of composure while being stared at by four hundred grey-faced zombies and we wonder why they're not smiling. I accepted that I, like everybody else on the plane, looked dead, and I ordered another beer.

The poor flight attendant. I remember when I was a kid, and my little sister was a little kid, and she, like most of her friends, wanted to be a flight attendant when she grew up (except we called them stewardesses then). Ah, the glamour of it! Jetting from capital to capital, serving he odd cocktail and flirting with the handsome captain. By the late teens, however, most girls begin to view the flight attendant as a high-altitude waitress, and the childhood dream fades in front of the disappointing reality.

There are some, obviously, who cling to the dream born in their youth, and they become the overly made-up automatons who push that cumbersome cart up and down the aisle throwing trays of rubber food at us just as we're falling asleep. And, invariably, halfway into any flight, they wear the same expression behind all the powder and too red lipstick which says, "Glamour, glamour, my queendom for some glamour!" Perhaps we should allow the little girls, like my sister of thirty years ago, who are still immersed in their romantic dreams, to serve us and keep us happy and laughing as we defy Mother Nature by flying and eating the inedible.

I recall the exact moment when it fully registered that I had left the United States. It was during a short refueling stop in Tahiti in which we passengers had roughly two hours to wander about the airport and stretch our legs and buy post cards and souvenirs.

As I stepped off the plane in the middle of the Tahitian night, I was hit in the face and lungs by a wave of warm, wet, heavy air that took me completely by surprise. It was like walking into a sauna. The tropical air stopped my where I stood. I looked about and grinned because I knew that my adventure had begun.

"Okay," I said to myself, "even though this is just an airport and Immigration won't let me leave the grounds, it is Tahiti and I'm going to get a taste of it." My taste of Tahiti consisted of eight laps around the inside of the tiny airport in as many minutes. I was avoiding the bar, which was situated right in the center, but my orbits around it were becoming progressively smaller until I finally splashed down on a bar stool.

There was simply nothing else to do. I ordered a beer from a native woman, found a comfortable seat where I could sit and watch the people circulate, drank my beer, and dozed off. I woke up a little later in one of those "Oh fuck, how long have I been asleep?" panics. I was just about to spring up out of my seat and run around asking strangers if I had missed my plane, when I spotted a familiar elderly woman from my flight.

"I'd recognize that flight face anywhere." I asked the nice lady if she'd mind making sure that I was awake when it came time for us to re-board our plane and she assured me that she would. I then turned my attention to the cat that was sleeping in my lap. What better place to sleep than on top of someone who's already sleeping? I certainly wasn't going to disturb her slumber since I was enjoying some of the same. I knew right away that she was a she because it was obvious that she was pregnant. Extremely pregnant.

I don't know what the normal gestation period is for cats, and I don't think she knew either because she looked long overdue. And although I had awakened in a panic, the feline mother-to-be remained asleep. I gently tapped her on the shoulder to wake her up. I didn't dare to try to lift her because I was scared I might squeeze out a few kittens. She slowly raised her head and looked at me, a bit condescendingly, as though perfectly aware of her motherly way and intent upon taking full advantage of it. She then lowered her head down onto my thigh and went back to sleep.

There was no way I could argue with that, so I surrendered and put my head back and rejoined the cat in slumber. When the nice elderly lady woke me up some time later, the big cat was gone. I checked my lap for any kittens and got up. So ended my Tahitian adventure.

I had one more stepping stone before Australia, at the Auckland airport, New Zealand. This was a true layover of fourteen hours and one which presented a dilemma. Should I go through customs, take a bus into Auckland and play around in town for the day? In a town that I would was scheduled to visit in six months anyway? Or should I stay in the airport, have a nice nap and drink beer with fellow travelers? I chose the latter and put a quick and painless end to my journey's first dilemma.

The first thing I did, however, was take a shower. It's amazing how a hot shower will remove even the most stubborn flight face. I felt refreshed and revived. But the only bit of luggage I had with me in New Zealand was my money belt. I, therefore, had to stand naked in the shower stall and drip-dry before putting on the same clothes I had donned the day before in Los Angeles. I hadn't realized that I wouldn't have access to my backpack and fresh clothes during my layover, but I was accustomed to making such oversights, so I just shrugged and slipped back into my lived-in laundry.

Upon stepping out of the shower room, I asked a friendly passer-by where I might find a cold New Zealand beer within the airport's perimeter. He pointed me in the right direction and I began a long, interesting day.

Not everyone you meet will be interesting. There are some people who can talk to you for hours, enthusiastic about who they are and what they've done, and bore you into

a deep depression. Others can be exciting without even saying a word. This variety is what gives life color for the people-
watcher like myself. Think of the birdwatcher. If every feath-
ered subject he viewed through his binoculars were a rare
Purple-Headed Bark-stripper, then they wouldn't be rare anymore, would they? He must sift through the countless common sparrows before discovering the elusive Bark-stripper
perched on a distant limb. He won't see one every time out,
but when he does it is an event quite special and one worthy
of celebration.

A dependable characteristic belonging to birds of a
feather dictates that they generally flock together; therefore,
it is not uncommon to find the rare Bark-stripper accompanied by one or more other Bark strippers seated at the same
table. These are the people who make all the watching and
waiting worthwhile, the human treasures who touch us within
and leave an everlasting impression. I had the honor of meeting a few such people on that long day in Auckland, the most
noteworthy being the members of the Robert Cray Band.

I met them in the bar over a few Steinlagers and had absolutely no idea who they were. It was not until we were an
hour into our conversation that I discovered that they were
an internationally famous band on their world tour. They told
me fascinating stories about their industry and what it was
like dealing with their ever-growing fame. I found it very intri-
guing how a group of basically normal young guys had gotten
together, pooled their talents, had become famous and were
now making large sums of money.

I liked them, admired them and envied them and, for these
reasons, I was racking my brain, trying to think of a way to
show them that I, too, possessed at least one artistic fiber in
my body. I longed to be a part of their fraternity. The only
thing I could think of which might demonstrate any artistic
potential I had was a poem I had written the night before

Thanksgiving (I feel I must admit that the poem would never have been written if I had been allowed into Hennessey's with the rest of my friends that night. I had been temporarily blacklisted for repeated misbehavior, so I sat at home alone and wrote the poem). To set the solemn tone of my poem, I looked each member of the band right in the eye and began my dramatic delivery.

BLACK NOVEMBER

When I was a Young Turkey, new to the coop,
My big brother Mike took me out on the stoop,
Then he sat me down, and he spoke real slow,
And he told me there was something that I had to know;
His look and his tone I will always remember,
When he told me of the horrors ... of Black November;
"Come about August, now listen to me,
Each day you'll get six meals instead of just three,
And soon you'll be thick, where once you were thin,
and you'll grow a big rubber thing   under your chin;
And then one morning, when you're warm in your bed,
In'll burst the farmer's wife and hack off your head;
Then she'll pluck out all your feathers so you're bald'n pink,and scoop out your guts and leave ya lyin' in the sink;
And then comes the worst part," he said, not bluffing,
"she'll spread your cheeks and pack your ass with stuffing."
Well, the rest of his words were too grim to repeat,
I sat on that stoop like a winged piece of meat,
And decided on the spot that, to avoid being cooked,
I'd have to lay low and remain overlooked;
I began a new diet of nuts and granola,
High-roughage salads, juice and diet cola;
And as they ate pastries and chocolates and crepes,
I stayed in my room doing Jane Fonda tapes;
I maintained my weight of two pounds and a half,

and tried not to notice when the bigger birds laughed;
But 'twas I who was laughing, under my breath,
as they chomped and they chewed ever closer to death;
And, sure enough when Black November rolled around,
I was the last turkey left in the entire compound;
So now I'm a pet in the farmer's wife's lap;
I haven't a worry, so I eat and I nap;
She held me today, while sewing and humming,
and smiled at me and said ... "Christmas is coming..."

While I didn't receive a standing ovation or a contract offer
from the Robert Cray Band, they did seem to be impressed
by my recitation and, for nearly a minute, I felt like one of
them.

"Damn, if I could only sing my poem they might even ask
me to accompany them on their world tour." My delusion
went undetected and quickly dissipated like a weak fart. We
shared another round of beers and then it was time for the
band to board their plane and move on to the next stop of
their concert tour. Just before they left, however, Dave Olson, the drummer, made me promise to send him a written
copy of my "fantastic" poem. Dave Olson: A Barkstripper
among Barkstrippers.

Soon thereafter, it was time for me to board one of the big
jets and make the final hop to Australia. The flight to Brisbane
would take about three hours, which gave me more than
enough time to formulate a plan as to what the hell I was
going to do once I landed in Australia. You see, there were
no instructions on the back of my plane ticket suggesting
what I do or which way I go upon arrival. Simple geography
would aid me slightly in making my decision because Brisbane is located on the East coast of the continent. My options
were thus reduced to heading North, South, or West. Trying
to be clever and sociable at the same time, I leaned to my

left and got the attention of a chubby, teenaged boy across the aisle from me. He was alone. I had automatically assumed that he was an over-fed Australian kid on his way home and that he might be able to give me a few pointers and suggestions on what to see and do in his home country.

"Excuse me," I said. "If you were going to Australia for the first time, where would you go?" Up to this point, I had only seen the kid in profile, and he was clearly round and blubbery. But when he turned and looked at me straight on, I was shocked by the width of his face -- like an image in a funhouse mirror, he was squatty and cartoonish. And set deeply in the folds between his forehead and those big, spherical cheeks, were two dark, little pig eyes. And below them, in the center of all that pink flesh, was his perfect little pig nose and a pig mouth. I was absolutely amazed by how much he resembled a pig. By the time he opened his mouth to speak, I had already made up my mind that he was going to squeal at me. He didn't. But what he did do was even more disturbing. He spoke with a very strong Bronx accent. Oh, the horror of it!

"This is my first time," he answered snottily, "Ain't been there yet. I'm going to Darwin, at the top where the crocodiles are. Then I'm gonna shoot some of 'em so I can take the skins."

My first impulse was to make an unkind remark about his taking the skin and then eating the rest of the crocodile, but I refrained. Instead, I said "That's illegal. If you kill a crocodile they'll arrest you and put you in jail."

"No they won't," replied the fat little shithead to my left. "My father's a diplomat, so I can do whatever the hell I want."

"I hate this kid," I thought. "I really hate him. And not just because he looks like a pig." I didn't say another word to him. I just turned away in amazement. I then imagined, in delightful clarity, a headline in the following week's national news-paper: "AMAZING PIG-BOY BECOMES BANQUET MEAL FOR HUNGRY CROCS"; and I wore a sinister smile.

Still in need of some pre-landing advice, I flagged down my favorite flight attendant and asked her where she thought I should go. I explained first, however, that I didn't wish to start off in one of the major metropolitan areas like Sydney or Melbourne.

"Do you like girls?" she asked.

My left eye twitched. "Yes, I do."

"Then you should go to Surfer's Paradise. It's only about an hour south of Brisbane. It's really good there and there are heaps of girls. They'll love your accent."

Well, that's all it took. I wouldn't be needing any more ad-vice. She had said the magic words: "It's really good there." First stop: Surfer's Paradise.

THREE

Anonymous

My arrival in Australia was rather anticlimactic because it was after midnight and I had suffered a serious relapse of flight face. My bones were weary and my feet were heavy. But a strange phenomenon began to lift my spirits. As I walked through customs and faced the crowd of Australians waiting for their loved ones, I knew, of course, that there wouldn't be anybody there to greet me. But I never truly realized until that moment that there wasn't a single person on the entire continent – or even in the hemisphere - who knew who I was or that I was there. I was so completely anonymous that I felt almost invisible.

Anonymity can certainly be a lonely state, but it is also one which offers a rare sort of freedom - a freedom which I found boundless and exciting. Anything I wanted to do, I would do. Nobody else had any say.

I looked at Australia in front of me and felt like I was six years old and looking at a new jar of peanut butter. When I was a kid and my mom wasn't around to make me a sandwich for lunch, I, like most kids, would climb on a chair and reach for the peanut butter. If it were a new jar and I was opening it for the first time, I would pause and behold the smooth, untouched surface. Sometimes I would look at it for quite a while, for, although I was hungry, I didn't want to spoil something so perfect. Then I would stick my finger in it (never the knife first). I was always very careful to avoid letting my big brother know that I held an untouched jar of peanut butter, because he would grab it from me and stick his finger in it before I had a chance and I would cry. But this time I was alone in the kitchen. I looked at the smooth, untouched surface of Australia and stuck in my finger.

A bus schedule told me that the next coach to Surfer's Paradise would be leaving from the airport at 8:45 a.m. I took a nice, long shower, put on a clean pair of shorts and a t-shirt (at last!), curled up in a corner and spent my first night unnoticed in Australia.

I never used to wake up early unless I had a job interview or I had to go to court. But a little voice in my head told me to wake up at six that morning. I told that little voice that he was obviously speaking into the wrong head and that if I found out where he was hiding, I was going to make sure that he never woke anybody up again. It was no use trying to go back to sleep, so I got up, had another shower, and ate breakfast. Then the little voice had the nerve to speak up again.

"See those two guys sitting over there?"

"Yeah, I see 'em. Why?"

"Do you see what they're drinking?"

"Yes. They're drinking what looks like very cold beer."

"That's right. Looks good, doesn't it, Dave?"

"Well, I suppose it does look pretty good, but it's only 7:30 in the morning."

"Sure, it's only 7:30 here, but it's 3:30 in the afternoon in L.A., and your body is definitely still running on L.A. time, isn't it, Dave?"

"Oh yeah, I guess it is ..."

"And don't forget, Dave, you're in Australia. Every day is a celebration when you're in Australia. Think of Paul Hogan from that Foster's commercial."

"Paul Hogan... he's a pretty cool guy ..."

"Yes, he is. And what do you think he would do if he were here?"

"I guess he'd probably go over there and have a couple beers with those guys ..."

An hour later I gulped down my fourth pint with the two friendly Swedish guys at the bar and said, "See ya around." It was time for me to catch my bus to Surfers Paradise. I found the right one, tossed my backpack into the luggage compartment underneath, climbed aboard, and stopped — confused. I then turned to the bus driver, who was seated behind the wheel which was situated on the wrong side of the bus. It was not the fact that the steering wheel was on the right side which had me confused; it was the fact that I couldn't see the bathroom and there had to be one.

"Where's the bathroom?" I asked him.

"The toilets are inside next to the ticket counter, but you'll have to hurry because..."

"No, no," I interrupted, "I mean the bathroom on this bus. I don't see it."

"That's because there isn't one, Mate."

I became very nervous. I didn't have to pee yet, but I had close to a gallon of just chugged Foster's fizzing in my belly. "How long will this drive take?" I asked.

"An hour and forty-five minutes, if the traffic's not bad."

I heard a little giggle. It was that fucking little voice. He knew all along that there was no bathroom on the bus. I'd been tricked.

Forty minutes later, I was in a cold sweat in seat 11a. All humor had left my life. The clock at the front of the bus told me that I had one hour and five minutes to go before I could go to the bathroom, "If the traffic's not bad." My bladder, how-ever, told me that I had four minutes, tops, and it wasn't con-cerned with traffic. I had stopped blinking after thirty-five minutes because it hurt. Suddenly, I heard the little voice say:

"Just let it go. Just pee, right where you sit, in seat 11a. Nobody will know it was you. And even if they did, who gives a shit? You're anonymous, remember? I only suggested that you have a beer with those guys. You're the lush who de-cided to have a fucking party at 7:30 in the goddamn morn-ing. Now your bladder is full. In fact, it's stretched beyond capacity, isn't it, Dave? One more good bump in the road and it's flood city anyway, so why not do it with some pride and just let it go right now? Just relax and let it go. Relax... pee... pee..."

"No!" I slowly rose from my seat and hobbled like a ninety-year-old man toward the front of the bus. I saw the driver looking at me in his big rear-view mirror as I limped up to him.

"Excuse me," I said, without moving my lips, "This is a very serious matter. If you don't stop this bus and let me out within thirty seconds, I'm going to pee all over myself and perhaps all over you and the rest of the passengers as well." He took one look at me, saw that I was serious, and said,

"Right. There's a big tree just ahead where you can do your business."

He pulled right over, I got out and, somehow, willed myself behind the tree. And life began again for me.

Five minutes later, I sprang out from behind that beautiful tree, did a pirouette and skipped weightlessly back onto the bus. The passengers, about whom I'd completely forgotten in my agony and self-pity, rose to their feet and gave me a standing ovation. I smiled, bowed and put my hands up in a humble gesture indicating that I wasn't really deserving of all that applause.

I had left my anonymity behind the tree next to an impossibly large puddle and, for the next sixty minutes, I was "the brave young man who had dared to stop the bus for a pee."

Kind Mr. Bus driver proved to be as punctual as he was empathetic and we rumbled into Surfer's Paradise right on time. When he had finished unloading the luggage from beneath the coach, I approached him and discreetly passed him a ten-dollar bill, which he accepted with equal discretion.

"What's that for, Mate?" he asked.

"Part of me will always love you for what you did. Thanks for stopping the bus." I then shook his hand, strapped my load onto my back, and headed for the beach.

I use the phrase "headed for the beach" loosely, for, in actuality, I did not head for the beach at all. It seems that some people are born with a compass in their head and they always know which way to go when it comes to decision time at the fork in the road. I don't care for these people. I was born without a needle on my compass and, therefore, have spent a considerable portion of my life wandering aimlessly. Surfer's Paradise is basically a thin strip of high-rise hotels fringing a straight beach. It is visible from miles away and anybody could see that on one side of the strip was the sea, and on the other side was the continent of Australia. Even I knew that. But my sense of direction, or the lack thereof, was preventing me from finding the beach.

I considered asking someone for directions, but decided against it because I was sure that the person I would ask would have noticed that I had been wandering for half an hour and would certainly laugh when he or she discovered that what I had been looking for was the largest ocean on the planet. I continued wandering.

By this point in my life I had long since ceased to become annoyed when I found myself lost. It had become a normal and predictable state for me, like other normal and predictable states. When I failed to get enough sleep, I could expect to become tired. When I drank too much beer, I could expect to become drunk. And when I went looking for something, I could expect to become lost. I developed a very open-minded philosophy about my problem of living lost -- sort of a "stop and smell the roses" attitude.

If I didn't have to be at my destination by a certain time, then what's the big goddamn hurry anyway? I've discovered many interesting spots and found some great bars which I never would have come across had I known where the hell I was (although I've usually been unable to find these spots again). I've also found that asking directions is a fine and legitimate reason for approaching a strange girl on the street (By "strange girl," I don't mean a strange girl, I mean an unfamiliar one; although I must admit that I have approached some pretty strange girls, but haven't made a practice of it because they invariably give strange directions). But, as I said, I was too proud to ask for directions on that sunny day in Surfer's Paradise and I was intent upon finding the sea by myself. And after forty minutes of search, I turned a corner and there it was — the elusive Pacific.

As I faced the water with the sand at my feet and the almost impervious wall of hotels at my back, I was a little surprised to see relatively few people on a vast beach, which stretched for miles in both directions. But then I remembered that it was still relatively early in the morning and figured that most people were in their rooms doing whatever people on vacation do when it's relatively early in the morning. It was infinitely difficult for me to choose a spot on which to bask, for there were an infinite number of spots available; each one looking just a little more enticing than the one next to it.

I closed my eyes and threw a coin high into the air, intent upon setting my day-camp wherever the coin landed. A few seconds later I opened my eyes and realized that there was no way I could tell where the coin had gone because my eyes had been closed. It was at this point that I realized that I was approaching delirium. I had been drinking far too much beer between intermittent, interrupted, unsatisfying naps for the past two days, and real sleep seemed like a long-lost lover with whom I was about to be reunited. I staggered forward a few steps and dropped my pack. I then pulled off my shirt, kicked off my shoes, threw down a towel and eased into the beckoning arms of slumber.

I'll guess and say that it was two o'clock when I woke up. Actually, I didn't wake up, somebody woke me up. I'm sure that I would have slept for several more hours had she not nudged my leg.

"I'm sorry to wake you..."

("Do I know this girl?")

"I've only done it because you haven't moved since I arrived, and I think you may be getting a burn."

("Where the hell am I?")

"Do you understand me? Do you speak English?"

("What's wrong with this picture? This girl is not wearing a shirt, that's what. I'm looking directly at her tits.")

"Are you awake now? I think you should turn over or move out of the sun."

I began to speak.

"Yeah, thanks... I guess I fell asleep."

"There's an understatement. It wasn't easy waking you up." Her accent was beautiful. She turned and walked back over toward her towel, twenty feet away.

"Thank you," I called after her, "you're very nice."

"No worries," she assured me over her shoulder. As she walked away from me, I wondered briefly about the possibility of the existence of God. Not because this was a religious experience for me, but because if he did exist, he was certainly laughing at me.

When I pulled my eyes off of the topless girl who had so pleasantly handed me my consciousness, I saw that the once empty beach had filled up when I was sleeping and was now covered with glistening, brown bodies. And most of these bodies belonged to glistening, brown girls; nearly all possessing and displaying— you guessed it— glistening, brown breasts.

My first impulse was to let out a hysterical giggle, like a parched man wandering across the desert who's just come to the top of the millionth dune to see a shimmering pool of cool water just on the other side. But then I stopped and reminded myself that one of the main reasons I had left home was my unhealthy obsession with females.

"Alright, let's slow the world down here for a minute and regain control. Okay... there are beautiful women all around me. I can clearly see their breasts. I have this urge to get up and touch every single one of them, but that's the old me talking. What are breasts, anyway? They're just mounds of fat which contain the mammary glands. Every female has them. Even Mom. The fact that I view them as sexual objects is merely a product of my home culture. But I have left home and must, therefore, not judge what I see here by my own American standards. I have to adapt.

Obviously, the breast is not viewed as a sexual object here in Surfer's Paradise, Australia, but rather as a part of the local scenery, like roses in the public gardens. I must shed my American lenses and view the bodies on this beach just as a native would. This is the first real test of my adventure, and I will pass it. I'll be okay, because they're just glands. Glands are all they are..."

That was when the little voice woke up and took a look around...

"Holy shit! Look at all the tits! My god, Dave, we're in heaven, and it's just like I always knew it would be... Tits everywhere. Quick, get up and mingle!"

"No! Stop it. They're just glands."

"'Glands'? What are ya, some kind of homo? They're tits."

"Mammary glands."

"Tits."

"They're like roses. I can appreciate them for their aesthetic value."

"Okay, fine. They're roses. So, let's go gather us a bouquet."

I closed my eyes and fought an inner battle of epic proportions. I called in every reinforcement I had — good manners, morals, honest intentions — all the five-star generals. But I was still outnumbered. The little voice got a bunch of hormones to help him and I was suffering some serious losses. Finally, I was forced to surrender. The battle was over. The test had ended. I had a boner.

I flipped over onto my stomach because I had already gotten far too much sun on the front half of my body and also because I was afraid I might be arrested for public indecency on my first day in Australia. I stewed in my shame with my head in my hands. But then I slowly began to come to my own defense. Nobody had warned me that the girls there wouldn't be wearing tops to their bikinis. I simply had not been prepared and my culture shock manifested itself in the form of an erection. I was soon convinced that it could have happened to any normal, virile young man and I, thereby, dismissed myself from guilt.

It was on that same beach in Surfer's Paradise where I first officially recognized the existence of "the little voice" and developed my theory about it. I concluded that we all harbor one. Everybody. The fat guy visiting the bakery may only buy two chocolate eclairs and a pecan pie, but the little voice in his head is urging him to buy a partnership with the baker so he can have a key to the front door. Anybody who's found a wallet full of cash has certainly had a chat with his or her little voice, even if they're honest and have every intention of returning it to its owner intact. The silent suggestion would be loud and clear: "Pocket the dough. Just tell 'em it was empty when you found it. Nobody will ever know the truth except me and you," (the little voice generally uses poor grammar when he speaks because he always slept during English class -- unless, of course, you were taking a test. Then he would be wide awake and pressuring you to look at your neighbor's paper).

After giving it much thought, my grand conclusion was that, if I was to become the man I had set out to be, I was going to have to come to terms with the little voice in my head. I didn't wish to shut him out completely because he may have something of value to suggest now and then. It was, after all, his little voice which prompted Sir Edmund Hillary to tough out the last leg of his heroic expedition to the top of virgin Everest.

Apparently, Edmund had had enough and was ready to give up just two hundred meters below the summit and head back to camp for afternoon tea, but the little voice in his head reminded him of all the talk shows he'd be on if he'd just make it to the peak. And, so he did. It suddenly became quite clear to me that what separates the men from the boys is knowing when to listen to the little voice and when to put your hand over his little mouth. I had finally realized what my dad had meant when he told me, time after time, to "exercise a little restraint."

Before that moment, I had never been able to figure out what the hell it was I was supposed to restrain. *A landmark self-discovery*

A weathered old man with a metal detector startled me out of my daydream when he stopped right next to my towel and blocked my sun. I watched him swing the disc-shaped head of his coin finder back and forth across the sand, listening for fortune to beep in his headphones.

He was obviously onto something, for the arc of his sweep was becoming shorter and shorter, until coming to a stop just four inches from my towel... which raised an interesting question in my mind: Where does my "space" end? At the edge of my towel? Or does my territory extend into a zone around my towel, like the few miles in the waters off of a sea-side country which foreign boats may not fish without first asking for permission? What if this man's little meter went crazy when he accidently passed his detector right over my towel? Could he ask me to move? Could he start a few feet away and tunnel right underneath me? What if I refused to move, he tunneled under my towel and found a treasure chest full of gold and silver bars? Would I be entitled to half? He'd probably wait until the sun went down so I'd get cold and leave before he'd reveal his discovery, the thieving old bastard. He began digging in the beep spot with a wire-mesh French fry scoop, and came up with three cigarette butts and a shiny coin, which he examined closely with squinted eyes.

"Wha'd you find, and ancient gold doubloon?" I pried.

"Nah. It's a 1987 American five-cent piece and, judging by your accent, mate, I reckon it belongs to you."

He flipped the nickel to me and continued on with his metal detecting. He didn't hear me say "thanks" because his old ears were busy again beneath the headphones. I was relieved to know that there was tangible proof that I had indeed thrown a coin into the air and amused that I had unknowingly placed my towel where it had landed. I put it in my pocket and decided it was time for me to get up and find myself a place to stay.

FOUR

Room #11

B ack amongst the high rises, I began asking people on the street where I might find cheap accommodation. I approached approximately six people and received approximately twelve suggestions. I nodded and smiled as they pointed and suggested and then I wandered in my pleasantly oblivious way until I came upon a haven for non-wealthy, ground-level travelers like myself called the "Backpackers United." The sign in the office window read "12.00 Dollars per Night. Share Accommodations. Bedding Provided." I signed in and paid for three nights in advance. The owner, a seemingly indifferent man of about thirty, took me on a brief tour.

The place was obviously once a motel, but it had been elbowed aside and into a state of premature obsolescence by the shiny new towers of glass and steel which had sprouted between it and the sea. No longer marketable as a motel, it had most likely changed hands and been demoted to the humble rank of "hostel;" its single and double beds carried away and replaced with bunk beds which would allow the new owner to stack the customers and put the place back into the black.

He showed me the pool, which was green. "I can't see the bottom," I told him.

"For twelve dollars a night, you'll be lucky to see the bottom some time. If I could charge twenty, you'd see the bottom." He then handed me my bedding and my key and pointed to a room on the second level.

The door to Room #11 was wide open, so I walked right in. The top bunk next to the window was the only one of the four which was bare of linen, so I guessed that it was mine. The other three were empty, but lived-in, so I figured that my roommates were out for the day. The floor was decorated with clothes, sand, beer bottles and various fast-food containers and the room was filled with a sweet, heavy, "party last night" smell. The only piece of furniture, other than the bunk beds, was a single metal chair which stood next to the wall. It looked as though it had once been mangled by a drunk and then crudely bent back into the shape of a chair the next morning when sobriety returned. There was a four-foot length of board bracketed to the right side wall which was installed to serve as a shelf or writing surface, but had ended up as a convenient place to put empty beer bottles and pizza boxes. Also on the shelf/desk was a glass containing the largest cockroach I had ever seen or heard about.

Whoever caught him wanted to keep, him, for there was a paperback book on top of the glass to prevent him from making an escape. Sharing the floor space of the cell with the big roach were several small pieces of food and candy, and a tiny toy motorcycle. Looking at the poor little prisoner, my first thought was "how do they expect him to ride his motorcycle with all that shit in his way?"

I looked around at the state of the room and considered picking up all the bottles and trash, but decided against it because I didn't wish to make a bad first impression by appearing on the scene as the "Felix Unger" type; especially since

I had always identified with Oscar Madison and if I were to clean up, I would be grossly misrepresenting myself.

I had always been a slob. Becoming a neater person was one of my sub-goals, falling under the grand heading of "growing up," but this was not the proper time to start. I settled for making my bed and organizing my section of the little room. I felt quite at home in Room #11 and I looked forward to meeting my roommates.

The solar overdose to which I had subjected myself on the beach was beginning to make itself known to me. I looked at my reflection in the small mirror which hung on the wall over the shelf/desk and I appeared much pinker than I had been the last time I had checked. I pressed my open hand firmly against my bare chest and then pulled it away, leaving behind a perfect white hand print which quickly disappeared into the pink without leaving a trace. "Shit," I said aloud, "I've been here for six hours and I've already got a goddamn sunburn." The unrelenting sun had also left me with a headache and a serious case of the chills. My teeth began to chatter. One would think that the human body would have evolved to the point by now where it would look out for its own best interests and show itself some mercy. Why, then, would my body allow me to have a headache and clicking molars at the same time? I felt as though someone large and untalented were playing the xylophone directly on my brain, and all I wanted to do was climb onto my bunk and disappear beneath my pillow.

Roughly two hours later, just as the sun was going down, I was jostled out of my coma by some activity. My roommates had come home. I had my pillow on top of my head to muffle the sounds of the world and the pounding in my brain and when they had a look at me, I heard them giggle and shush each other and giggle some more. It was clear that they had been drinking and one of them plunged recklessly into the bunk beneath mine. I removed the pillow from my head, sat up stiffly and said "Hello, I'm Dave." The two standing looked at me, said "hello," and began giggling again. They clearly found my appearance amusing. "What's so funny?" I asked.

The taller of the two answered in a strong French accent, "I am sorry. We are sorry. You have too much of the sun, yes?" I smiled and nodded, "Yes. I am a stupid American asshole."

They both laughed enthusiastically at this and I heard some weak laughter from the bunk below me as well. The tall one spoke again,

"You are very red and your eyes are very big." *"My eyes are very big?"* I wondered what the hell he meant, so I jumped down from my bunk onto rubbery legs to have a look in the mirror.

My eyelids had gotten sunburned along with the rest of my front half, and were now puffed like little pink pillows. I looked so pathetic that all I could do was laugh. And when my cheery roommates saw that I was laughing at myself, they joined right in with me.

I liked my roommates. The two giggly ones were not French, but Swiss. The tall one called himself Jack, and the shorter, quieter one went by Nick. Both were in their early twenties.

The one in the bunk below mine was Miles, twenty-five and very English. The alcohol had obviously gotten the better of him and he was embarrassed.

"I'm really very sorry if we woke you, I'm usually not like this. These two Swiss bastards got me drunk." More laughing. Jack handed me two ice cubes from the cooler they had come in with and suggested that I put them on my eyes. As I was about to do so, he said "But first drink" and handed me a plastic two-liter coke bottle which was 3/4 full.

"What's in it?" I asked.

"Bourbon," he answered.

"You guys didn't drink very much."

Nick reached into the cooler and produced two empties of the same size and proudly held them up for me to behold.

"Oh, I see," I said.

He then grinned and pointed the empties at Miles who had just fallen asleep, fully clothed, with his face buried in his pillow. The three of us laughed and I took a big chug from the bottle. I hadn't realized until that moment how dehydrated I was. The drink was icy cold with a bold suggestion of bourbon, and I had to force myself to stop gulping it.

An hour later I took the last swallow that the bottle had to offer. At my Swiss friends' insistence, I had drunk nearly all of it myself and, although it had been only lightly laced with bourbon, it had given me a mild, pleasant buzz and taken the edge off my aches and pains. Jack, Nick, and I moved out onto the veranda and talked for quite a while. I told them that I had visited their country when I was eighteen during a seven-week tour of Europe with a buddy, but that I remembered very little because, at that age, my mind was still an amorphous ball of swirling vapors and that absorbing and appreciating a foreign culture was still far beyond me. Neither of them had ever visited the United States and Jack asked me, "What is America really like?" That was a toughie and I struggled for an answer. When I found out that they had seen "Leave it to Beaver" on Swiss television, I explained to them that America was just like that and that I was a lot like Eddie Haskell.

Several others drifted out of their rooms or returned from daily outings and joined us on the veranda. Soon we numbered over a dozen, with representatives from all over the world. This was a situation I had not anticipated. When I had set out for Australia, I naturally expected to enter a world of Australians. There, making up a circle of fourteen, sat visitors from Germany, Switzerland, Sweden, England, Canada, Japan, just two Australians, and I, the sole American.

Well into the international conference, I realized that I had been taking for granted the fact that everybody was speaking English. I felt a bit guilty because they had all taken the time and trouble to master English, while my knowledge of foreign languages, other than a little California Spanish, was limited to "one beer please" in German, and all I could say with confidence in Japanese was "yes" and "good-bye."

The common denominator of "travel" made the conversation eager, warm and easy flowing. Many or most in the circle had been traveling for months and the colorful stories of peoples and cultures encountered along the way made me excited and proud to be a new member of this fraternity of nomads.

The drink of the budget traveler, I quickly learned, was wine; not by the bottle, but by the box. Many drank the wine by preference, but most had purchased the four-liter casks because they were, by far, the most economical means of getting drunk. There were eight casks on the veranda — thirty-two liters of cheap white wine. Someone handed me a cup and I sampled a bit from each cask. They were of several different brands and varieties and, although I was mainly a beer drinker and about as far away from being a wine connoisseur as a guy can be, even to my palate they tasted like they were grape juice one day and then wine the next. No ageing here, we're talking about wines which are judged in terms of freshness. A comparison which came to mind was the difference between real and processed cheese, but I've always been partial to Velveeta, so I thought the wine was quite tasty and I gulped it as enthusiastically as the rest of the group.

As midnight approached, the casks began to run dry, and, thus, our numbers began to dwindle. I witnessed several times the inevitable ritual task of removing the foil bladder from the box when the wine was down to a few precious drops and then actually wrung into the glass.

Nick and Jack decided that they had had enough fun for one day and they retired to their bunks. I told them that I would be following soon. The fact that it was my first night in the country gave me an adrenal edge over the others and, although I did my best to keep the conversation going, my foreign friends were dropping one by one. It wasn't long before the circle had become a line, and I sat facing the night's only other survivor.

He was a smiling Japanese fellow named Kenji who had become over-wined very early and had stopped grinning for an hour, but had since sobered up and was, once again, displaying his impressive set of teeth. Our conversation flowed at a trickle because every word of Kenji's English had to be unearthed from his memory and he had an amusing habit of digging up the wrong one. But he labored along admirably and we had fun and were proud of ourselves when we had completed a sentence together and arrived at a mutual conclusion.

Soon, however, Kenji, too, succumbed to the hour and at 2 a.m., said, in his practiced English, "Goodnight, David, I will see you tomorrow." I answered proudly, in my best and only Japanese,

"Yes, good-bye."

After visiting the bathroom, I did my best to navigate the floor of room #11 as quietly as I could in the dark, but my efforts were futile and I clinked bottles and crinkled potato chip bags all the way across the room. I stopped to listen when I reached my bunk, and was relieved to hear that I hadn't disturbed any of the deep, rhythmic breathing which filled the room. It was, however, to be the last peaceful moment of the night for the four of us.

I stood facing my bunk in the dark and wondered how I could best climb up without disturbing Miles, who lay snoring below. It wasn't terribly high, about shoulder level, but there was no step ladder and no visible foothold to give me any leverage on the way up. I didn't want to put my feet on Miles' mattress, so I chose to place my right foot against the right, near-side vertical support bar while pulling myself up with my arms across my mattress. This nearly worked and I almost had my left knee up, when I quite suddenly lost my toe grip on the bar.

Because I was draped with my chest and chin holding me, up on the upper bunk, my feet did not drop to the floor when I slipped. Instead, they swung, with great velocity, across the lower bunk and my right foot came to rest with half of my weight on the center of Miles' face. There was a heavy slap, followed by a muffled scream as poor Miles pushed my foot off of his mouth and scrambled from his bunk in terror. I knew instantly that he had no idea what had just happened and I tried to stop him and tell him that everything was alright. But, in the confusion, I couldn't think of his name and, because it was so dark, the hand I had reached out to put on his shoulder found the middle of his face instead. He screamed again, this time hysterically,

"Somebody help me! He's killing me!" Again, I tried to console him, but in his panic, he shoved me aside and rushed past me. I will never forget the series of sounds which followed.

First there was the expected clinking of bottles bouncing off of one another, then a cry, then a heavy thud, a grunt, a gurgle, a wretch, the unmistakable sounds of a man throwing up, another man screaming, another wretch, lots more throwing up, and then total chaos.

Seconds later I was searching for the light switch, but somebody beat me to it and the room was suddenly bright. It was Jack who had gotten there first and he stood wearing his underwear and an expression of total bewilderment. The smell of throw-up was nauseating, but there wasn't nearly as much of it on the floor as I expected. Certainly, all of the gurgling and retching I had heard would have produced more than the measly patch which lay glistening on the carpet. I then followed jack's look of shock and total disbelief across the room to Nick and discovered that the rest of it had come to rest on his sheets and his person.

It clung stubbornly to his pajamas from chest to ankle. Sitting on the edge of his bed with his feet on the floor, he looked straight at me, then at Jack, shook his head, and convulsed into an impressive dry-heave. Miles then emerged from the bathroom toweling wet hair and, together, we began to assemble the pieces of the shattered night.

Miles rarely drank alcohol because it didn't sit well in his belly and it made him sleepy. On this particular occasion, he had fallen asleep before his stomach had become upset and he lay oblivious to the fact that his guts were churning. He also happened to be having a bad dream about a crazy man chasing him down the beach with a cricket bat. That was the point at which I had stepped on his face. Still half-dreaming, he had flown from his bed in terror only to run into a dark figure of a man trying to put a hand over his mouth. He screamed for help and fled into the darkness. On his first full stride, however, his foot had landed roundly on a beer bottle which rolled, slipped, and squirted away. An instant later he found himself parallel with, and four feet above, the floor. The thud, which we all clearly heard, led to the grunt and, because of the state of his stomach, led also to the gurgle, the wretch, and the unmistakable sounds which followed.

Having just been thrust into a world of shock and violence, poor, poor Miles' last concern was the direction in which his mouth was pointing when his body decided it was time to rid itself of unwelcome bourbon. Nick gave new meaning to the term "rude awakening" when, just as he was sitting up to see what all the commotion was about, a torrential shower of vomit rained on him out of the darkness. When the scent registered and he realized what the warm substance was, a second, more powerful wave blasted him in the chest. Quite involuntarily, and without a trace of contempt, Nick then leaned to his left and projected the contents of his own stomach onto Miles, who was seated on the floor next to Nick's bed and who, until that moment, was just beginning to feel the comforting hand of recovery. At this last assault upon his sanity, Miles whimpered once, threw up on Nick's legs, got to his feet, and rushed to the bathroom.

On the following morning, the four of us were able to laugh about the previous night's fiasco, but it was clear, even to me, the newcomer, that the relationships of the day before were forever changed. Miles was able to smile at me through swollen lips, but I could see the resentment in his eyes and, even after apologizing to him half a dozen times, I knew that I would never be forgiven for my loss of footing which had led to the most horrific sixty seconds of his life. But, as strange as it may sound, some good did emerge from the midnight mayhem.

While my relationship with Miles had certainly taken a sharp turn for the worse, Nick and Miles now shared a unique closeness as a result of having thrown up on one another. Not unlike blood brothers, they had cemented a rare manly bond, and had thus become the only barf brothers I had ever met.

I spent the next week exploring with my roommates and, together, we saw all there was to see of Surfer's Paradise — which, in actuality, was not a paradise for surfers at all. The sea was frothy, wind-blown and chaotic, and the few surfers I did see were being tossed about like rodeo bull riders. After giving much thought to the blatant misnomer, I concluded that, when the city was in its infancy, a tourism-minded entrepreneur called a town meeting and proposed using the title to lure wealthy beach lovers from around the world.

"I know you're all wondering why I've called you here, and now I'm going to tell you. I hereby propose that we henceforth refer to our humble beach-side settlement as 'Surfer's Paradise'." A round man with a red face removes his floppy hat as he rises from his seat in the rear of the hall.

"I'm not sure I heard you right, mate. Did you say 'Surfer's Paradise'?"

"Yes I did. I said Surfer's Paradise." The room is suddenly filled with the unintelligible murmurings of the crowd, like in an old courtroom movie when the key witness testifies that he heard the accused say, on the very night of the gruesome murder, "*If I had my axe with me, I'd chop that bastard into three-inch cubes.*" The murmuring subsides as another concerned citizen rises to voice his opinion on the issue.

"Correct me if I'm wrong, but the waters off our shore are frothy, wind-blown, and chaotic. The only man I've ever seen surfing here was an asshole. I understand your intention of luring wealthy beach lovers from around the world to stiffen our flaccid tourism industry, but I'm afraid they might be awfully disappointed once they got here..."

While I can't deny that I had fun in Surfer's Paradise, the city was certainly not what I expected and I did not yet feel as though I had arrived in Australia. It was a generic tourist Mecca which represented Australian culture about as much as Honolulu represents that of old Hawaii. To be completely truthful, though, I must admit that I was simple and rather shallow and that it was not the absence of legitimate, unspoiled Australian culture which disappointed me most about Surfer's Paradise.

The major disappointment for me was the fact that I had been on the continent for over a week and I had yet to see a kangaroo. Simple men require simple pleasures. I simply wanted to see a kangaroo. I wanted to see him hopping. I wanted to see him hopping in unison with his friends. Boing, boing, boing. I disclosed this simple dream of mine to my companions and roommates at the hostel and discovered that this was a commonly held longing.

As spokesman for this international group of thrill seekers, I approached Gary, a local in his mid-twenties who slept in his car by night and spent part of every day socializing at the Backpackers United with us transients and I asked him if he'd mind driving us to an area where we'd be likely to view some kangaroos. He was a pleasant fellow and gladly agreed, as long as we would pay for the "petrol." He then neatened up his bedroom, the gang piled in and we set off on our quest.

The kangaroo, I was told, is not a beach goer (I wondered why, so I had done a few experiments on my own and determined that hopping in sand is exceedingly difficult). Gary, being the only Australian in the car, informed us that we would be far more likely to see one if we were to move inland. As he drove, the rest of us scanned the hilly green fields and pastures on either side with cameras ready. It soon became obvious that Gary had absolutely no idea where we were or where we were heading, but this didn't bother any of us because being lost merely added to our growing sense of adventure.

Soon the hills became steeper and more pronounced, and we began to wonder if we were, perhaps, moving into territory which would not be conducive to kangaroo viewing. On any nature program I'd ever seen, the kangaroo was shown hopping across vast, arid plains.

Gary insisted that it is a very adaptable creature and he even recalled hearing about a rare species called the "Hill

Hopper" (Gary was a chronic liar, but a creative one). We stopped at a little, run-down petrol station to ask for advice when we found ourselves half way up a heavily vegetated mountain and a remarkably energetic, shriveled, little man buzzed out the door like a bee and was ready to fill our tank before we'd even come to a stop. Obviously, customers were a rare and welcome sight up there in the boondocks, but, unfortunately, we had filled up just thirty minutes earlier. I felt a pang of guilt when I saw the disappointment fill his eyes as he realized he would make no profit from us.

My guilt quickly evaporated, however, when I opened my mouth and said something ridiculous.

"Excuse me, sir, could you please tell us where one might go if one wanted to view a kangaroo? But before you answer that, I want to make it clear that we're not tourists." The clear-eyed, wizened, old Australian looked in through the windshield at the six of us gripping our cameras and smiled toothlessly.

"You didn't have to tell me that; anybody with half a brain could see that you're a bunch of locals." Nick and Jack raised their automatics simultaneously and snapped his picture.

"You're not likely to see any 'roos up here in the hills," he continued. "If I was you I'd go down to Kangaroo Park in Surfer's Paradise. There's hundreds of 'em there and they're tame enough to take food right out of your hands,"

"That place is for tourists," I said. "We'd rather see them in the wild, wouldn't we fellas?" Nick, Jack, Miles, Kenji, and Kazuo (Kenji's Japanese pal) all nodded in agreement.

"Are you telling us that there is absolutely no chance of seeing a kangaroo up here?" I continued. "Has a kangaroo never been seen here?"

"Well, maybe a couple Hill Hoppers, but it's been a long time." That was good enough for us. We felt that if we wanted to see one badly enough, then we would see one. Even if there was only one kangaroo on the entire mountain, our desire would attract him and he would happen by. He would then do something really cute and amazing for our benefit, and we would get some fine photographs. We drove a few more kilometers up the winding road, parked, found a narrow trail, and made our way into the rain forest.

This was the first time I had ever set foot in a real rain forest and I was awe struck almost to the point of forgetting why we were there. Massive, gnarled fists of knuckled roots gripped the forest floor all around us, like giant hands reaching down through the canopy above. Where the great trunks were visible through the ferns and mosses which nearly covered them, the wood glistened with moisture. We meandered along through the wet, green filtered light at a leisurely pace, stopping now and then to listen for hopping sounds. There were none.

Soon it began to rain-- a dependable characteristic of the rain forest. We felt none of the rain directly. The water would puddle on the leaves of the many layers of canopy above until becoming too heavy to be held and then fall on us in big, healthy drops. And still no sign of a kangaroo. We discussed the disappointing prospect that if there had been any kangaroo tracks to discover and follow, they would almost certainly be washed away by the rain.

Our faith was dwindling. Kenji said something in his labored English about his camera having water in it, so it was agreed upon that we return to the shelter of Gary's station wagon. As we retraced our steps along the narrow path, Miles was examining his camera for moisture when he halted quite suddenly and let out a loud wail. He held his hand out away from his body in horror and total disgust. We quickly gathered around him to see what his problem was. On the back of poor Miles' hand, right in the middle, clung a plump, black, shiny leach.

I believe that our first reaction as a group was a flash of pity for poor Miles. The definition of "Flash" in Webster's dictionary is "to blaze suddenly and die out." Our pity blazed suddenly and died out, making room for the more important individual concern for self. "If he's got a leech on him, then I might have a leech on me," is basically how we all felt as our eyes left him and we began examining our own bodies for leeches.

I've always considered myself a pretty masculine guy. Even tough, sometimes. I've played rugby for years and had more than my share of hard, physical contact without complaining. I've been in bar fights where I was punched squarely in the face. No real problem.

However, when I looked down and saw eight or ten leeches sucking blood from my white, skinny legs, I screamed like a little girl with a bee in her hair. There were leeches on all of us, and not just on the legs, but arms, shoulders, necks-- any bit of skin that was exposed. Evidently, they were on the leaves all around us and when it had begun to rain they fell on us in the big drops of water. Most of the leeches could simply be picked or rubbed right off, but some were stubborn and didn't want to let go.

We decided to drive back down to the petrol station and see if the old man could help us get them off. As Gary sped down the hill, we all sat motionless in a state of disgust. Nobody said anything. Poor Miles had two big juicy ones on the back of his neck and he sat wide-eyed and rigid as a board. The old station owner didn't emerge as quickly this time, but strolled out as we climbed stiffly from the car.

Miles was at the front and was uncharacteristically blunt.

"Give us something to get these fucking leeches off." The old man laughed so hard at Miles I thought he was going to collapse. He held his sides and doubled over.

"Made friends with a few leeches, did ya?"

"There's nothing funny about this," Miles snapped. "Can you help us get them off or not?"

"Sure, I'll get 'em off, just take it easy, mate, they won't hurt ya. A little salt'll take 'em right off."

"Do you have some salt you can give us?," Miles persisted.

"I've got some salt I can sell you."

"That's fine, just get it. And be quick about it, please. I'm starting to feel as though I could be sick."

Well, the old Aussie managed to get his profit after all when he stuck us for five bucks for a small shaker of salt. When I told him I thought the price was a bit high, he told us we could probably get it a lot cheaper at the next shop down the road, just thirty kilometers away.

Miles exclaimed that money was no object, paid the man and began frantically salting himself. Once salted, the leeches curled up and peeled right off and, once again, Miles was his proper self. The rest of us then took turns sprinkling ourselves and checking each other's backs for any that we may have missed. Only when the very last one was found and salted to death were we able to relax and even laugh about our misadventure.

FIVE

The Lioness

At the end of my second week in Surfer's Paradise, I was down to my last two hundred dollars. I had landed with eight hundred in my pocket and that was supposed to last me a month, but I failed to allow for realistic beer expenditures when I constructed my budget.

My plan all along was to re-stuff my backpack and hitchhike north when my funds had dwindled to the two hundred-dollar level. I would then settle any place along the coast which seemed comfortable, find work, and refill my money belt before moving on again. I figured that stopping to work periodically would not only keep my stomach full, but would also enable me to blend into local culture along the way and truly get to know the Australian people. Ready to move on, I began to say my good-byes and exchange addresses with my friends at the hostel, and I was only a day away from departure when I met Judith.

I had just returned from a late afternoon run on the beach, and I was enjoying a cold beer in the shade under the veranda with my Tasmanian friend Lawrence. "Lorie," as he preferred to be called, was the crudest man I had ever met. Sporting a shrub-like beard which hadn't seen the edge of a blade for years, Lorie equated body odor with manliness and felt that he was compromising his manhood when he succumbed to the pressures applied by his friends and roommates and took his Sunday bath.

Twenty-six years old but looking at least ten years older, this was a man who would save up his farts for special moments and let one go only if there were somebody around to appreciate it. Having just thunderously spoiled several cubic yards of air around himself, he would then judge his performance by what he called the "Scale of Humidity" and assign it a score anywhere along the scale from one to ten; a score of One was the driest possible and was what he called "a desert breeze," and a Ten meaning that he had actually shit his pants.

He explained to me that his scores varied from day to day according to his diet, but usually averaged around the Five range, which he called "Autumn Mist" (He boasted that he had actually scored a Ten on one occasion. He'd gone to the movies with his older sister and felt what he thought to be a great fart building up during the first half of the film. He waited patiently for the perfect moment and finally it arrived. It was during a touching funeral scene and Lorie claimed that one could have heard a pin drop in the packed theater. He leaned to his left to free his right cheek and allow for passage and gave it a strong push to make sure even the projectionist heard it. By the time he realized that it was more than just gas, the damage was done. Within thirty seconds, two-thirds of the audience had evacuated, including his sister who, Lorie bragged, was a world-class farter herself, and the odorous Tasmanian watched the rest of the movie alone).

The two of us were sitting and exchanging such anecdotal gems in the shade under the veranda when we both noticed two girls with packs walk up to the office to check in. Both were pretty, but one of them, I felt, was particularly attractive.

This was not the first girl to catch my eye in Australia. I had gotten close with three nice girls since my arrival (well, perhaps "nice girls" is the wrong phrase), but I was intent upon putting an end to my womanizing ways and I considered these three incidents to be unintentional lapses resulting from my celebratory mood. It was not my intention to cut out sex entirely, just the recreational sort where grunts outnumbered words.

Certainly, I was doing no harm by merely looking at this pretty girl who had just appeared. And, of course, it would be perfectly acceptable for me to introduce myself when she had finished checking in. There would be nothing wrong with that; this girl was obviously quite special.

It only took five minutes for the girls to take care of their business in the office and when they had finished, Paul, the seemingly indifferent owner-manager, walked them past us as he gave them the usual two-minute tour of the facilities (laundry room, t.v. room, green pool). I opened my mouth to say hello, but Lorie was faster. Allow me to explain that Lorie's view of women was not that of a civilized man. Born and raised in the back country of Tasmania, his idea of a good woman was one who was tough, beefy, had most of her teeth, and could chop wood. He didn't go for these frail, "city-type Barbie dolls" who wore make-up and shaved under their arms. When the two new arrivals walked past, he saw an opportunity to have a little fun.

"G'day, ladies, how about showin' us your pink bits?" The taller of the two girls, the one whom I found so attractive, stopped and stared at Lorie, not believing what she thought she had just heard him say. I stared at him too; I couldn't believe it either. The pretty brunette spoke to Lorie as though he were a child.

"I'm terribly sorry, I don't think I heard you correctly. What did you say?" Lorie was not in the least bit intimidated by her coolness because he knew that he was an animal with nothing to lose.

"How's your bum for spots?" he asked her. This girl was very British and equally impressive.

"You, sir, are a cretin in need of a bashing and a bath." Lorie wasn't going to let this obvious city girl have the last word. He leaned to his left and released an incredibly violent fart which sounded like a sail ripping under the force of a gale. He grinned and waited for her reaction, but this girl, whom I had so quickly come to admire, didn't even blink.

"You Australian men are so articulate. And I'll bet you were captain of your debate team."

"He's from Tasmania," I interjected, hoping that she would notice my accent and deduce that I was not from the same hemisphere as Lorie.

"That's right," Lorie added, "I'm from Tazzy." "And I'll wager that you broke many a young girl's heart when you left home," said the Lioness, pointedly.

"As a matter of fact," Lorie boasted, "I do have a certain female back at home who's probably in my bed thinking about me right now."

"Is that so?" she mused. "No doubt she's worried that you may burst in and beat her with a newspaper when you discover that she's jumped up onto your bed again."

I laughed. Lorie didn't. I think that this was the first time he had ever been defeated by a "mere female." He leaned to his left and tried his best to fart again, but even his trusty sphincter failed him. He slumped in his chair, a beaten man. The English girl turned, rejoined her partner and Paul (who had witnessed the entire slaughter with sympathetic male eyes), and they marched off.

I had to lie to Lorie when I left him twenty minutes later because I was going upstairs to meet the girl who had just made a fool of him and I felt I should tread softly on the cracked shell of the rough man's ego. It had not been so much what the girl had said to him, it was her delivery — her attitude of superiority and condescension which left him looking and feeling like a small, very dirty man. I found her confidence and self-assuredness to be extremely sexy and, as I scaled the stairs on the way up to her room, I was hoping that she hadn't connected me with what had happened.

Her partner answered my knock wearing an expression which said that she, for one, felt that I was in on the harassment conspiracy with that hairy, flatulent man under the veranda.

"Hello," I began, "I just wanted to make sure that there were no hard feelings for what happened downstairs."

"Is he your friend?" she asked, holding the door open only a few inches and effectively blocking my view into the room.

"Yeah, he's my friend. He's a great guy, really. He just isn't very refined."

"No, he isn't."

"May I come in for a minute and apologize to your friend, too?"

"I'll ask her," she said and closed the door. I could clearly hear her through the thin, cheap door as she spoke.

"It's that American Bloke from downstairs. He wants to know if he can come in and apologize." There were then sounds of muffled giggling from both of them and suddenly I was quite nervous. When the girl re-opened the door and faced me again, I was almost expecting her to say "M'lady is indisposed. Try again tomorrow."

Instead she said "Alright, you can come in, but only for a minute; we've been on a bus all day and we're both knackered" ("Knackered" was a new word for me, but in context I was able to figure out that it meant that they had Bus Face).

She opened the door and I entered. The room contained two sets of bunks, just, like #11; napping in the pair of bunks against the right-side wall were two Japanese girls, one above the other, each with her sheet tucked neatly up under her chin and lying as still and rigid as a cadaver (the Japanese even sleep politely). The girl I had come to meet was kneeling on the floor next to her open backpack organizing her clothes. Before I'd even had a chance to address her, she pointed to her dormant Asian roommates and then put her finger to her lips.

"Whisper," she said.

"Can you come outside for a minute so we don't have to?" I asked, whispering. Without answering, she stood and led me out the door. She sat down in a tired deck chair and I took the one across from her.

"I'm Dave from California," I began.

"I'm Judith from Manchester." She extended her hand and impressed me yet again, this time with her firm grip.

"That's a pretty strong grip you've got."

"I grew up with a younger brother who used to torment me every day until I would be forced to throttle him. He was a little shit, but now we're quite close." An awkward moment of silence followed. It was clear that she was expecting me to say what I had come to say.

"I came up here to apologize for what my friend said downstairs, but I'm just beginning to feel that there's really no need to."

"I don't understand..."

"I mean that you handled him and put an end to the problem right then and there. You took care of it yourself and made a fool out of him."

"Perhaps I owe that to my brother as well. He used to bring his school mates home with him and they usually proved to be about as charming as your friend downstairs."

"He is a bit rough around the edges," I admitted.

"He's a caveman," she opined.

"But a loveable one," I added. "I suppose the real reason I came up here was so that I could have my own chance to meet you without any interference."

"Why would you want to meet me?" she asked.

"Well, at first I wanted to meet you because you're very pretty; then, when I saw the way you handled Lorie, I realized that there was much more to you than just good looks."

"Thank you. You know, you're awfully American."

"Why am I awfully American?"

"You're so blunt. People from your country are always very blunt."

"Is that negative?"

"That depends on the individual. If an unfriendly person is blunt, then it's certainly negative. But if someone is nice and complimentary, like you, then it's okay. Sometimes it can be a little embarrassing..."

"Did I embarrass you? I didn't mean to."

"Oh, no. I wasn't embarrassed. The average English girl would probably be embarrassed by your approach, but I'm not normal."

"You certainly aren't," I observed.

"You see? Right there — an English fellow wouldn't say that. They're far subtler."

"I guess I'm just too impatient to be subtle. I think people miss too many good opportunities in life because of subtlety. Besides, I'm leaving Surfer's tomorrow and I'd kick myself if I left anything unsaid." I quickly scanned her face for any sign of disappointment about my leaving. I didn't see any.

"Where will you be going?" she asked.

"I'm not really sure. I want to make it up to Cairns eventually, but I'll be stopping any place along the way that I like and where I can find work."

"Are you taking a bus?"

"No, I'm hitch-hiking."

"Alone?"

"Yes."

"Haven't you heard about all the travelers who've disappeared hitching in the past few months? It's very dangerous." (She's concerned. I like it.)

"I'll be alright. It's nice to know that you're worried though," I said, smiling.

"I'm not worried. I'm sure you'll be fine."

"Not even in the subtlest sort of way? Remember, I'll be a stranger alone in a strange land." She smiled. "Well, perhaps I'd feel a little better if I knew that you were on a bus. But don't flatter yourself too much. I'd worry about your hairy farting friend, too, if he were hitching alone."

"But this time it happens to be me that you're worried about, and I'll take any attention I can get from you."

"Does it ever become tiresome being so forward? It must be exhausting."

"No, not at all. I think it's the other way around. It takes more energy to think of all the reasons not to say something than it takes to just say it. I find it easier to let thoughts and words flow without censoring them."

"That's an interesting point of view. Does it ever get you into trouble?"

"I suppose it has; but speaking my mind has gotten me into a lot more good situations than bad ones. Like this one -- this is a good situation."

"I suppose it could be a lot worse," she said, smiling again.

"Listen," I said. "I know that you and your friend are tired..."

"Heidi," she interjected.

"Oh, thanks. I know that you and Heidi are tired, or 'knackered'; why don't you go crash out for a couple of hours and when you wake up, I'll show you around Surfer's Paradise. I'll even buy you a beer."

"I prefer wine."

"Then I'll buy you a glass of wine. What do you say?"

"What about Heidi? Can she come along as well?"

"Of course. I'll even talk to Lorie and we can make it a double date."

(Laughing) "I think she'd prefer to have it just the three of us. Oh... I think I should tell you, I have a boyfriend."

"I'm sorry, that's where I draw the line -- he can't come."

"That's okay," she said. "He's in England."

"Well, it was thoughtful of you to tell me that, but it's really not necessary. I just want some friendly company."

"Good," she said, "So do I."

I spent the next couple of hours on my bunk reading a book by John Steinbeck called *Travels With Charley*. It was about a journey Mr. Steinbeck embarked upon around America to re-acquaint himself with his country, with which he felt he was losing touch. He observes several noteworthy Barkstrippers along the way and shares his adventures with his big, regal poodle named Charley, who looks down his nose at everything from the passenger seat of the truck.

Another backpacker had passed it along to me after reading it and I would do the same. The book inspired me in two ways; as a traveler, I was reminded of the importance of simply meeting the people, of sharing and comparing ideas and seeing the world from other perspectives; and as a writer -- Mr. Steinbeck was a master of the English language, but even more importantly, he was a master of his own mind and possessed the power to grasp and express feelings and insights which, to most writers, would almost instantly fade and disappear forever like wisps of smoke.

Watching a great athlete makes some want to get up and run; reading John Steinbeck made me want to sit down and write. Nick, Jack and Miles had moved on and gone their separate ways and, as far as I was concerned, had taken the magic of Room #11 with them.

In their places were a sleepy German guy who only left his bunk to eat and go to the bathroom and two Spanish drunks who were just as boring. The only familiar face remaining was on the big cockroach in the glass, and even he was beginning to lose his novelty.

Although I still had plenty of friends and acquaintances at and around the hostel, I felt that my best times in Surfer's Paradise had passed. And while I was content with my plan to leave on the following day, I harbored distressingly strong regrets about not having met Judith sooner.

Just as I was beginning to wonder if Judith had overslept or changed her mind about our evening plans, there was a tap at my open door and she glided across the threshold. The healthy, natural beauty she radiated evoked a strange reaction within me. I couldn't help but think about how much she would be resented in Los Angeles by all the make-up slaves who never leave the house without a liter-sized can of hair spray in their hand bag and who duck into the powder room every twenty minutes with their touch-up kit to make sure that the face that they'd applied that morning hadn't run or cracked (Perhaps someday the world will understand why so many girls of Los Angeles aspire to look like clowns. I'm still waiting for fashion trends to include funny pointed shoes with bells on them). She was tall and tan with eyes like dark chocolate.

Her thick, brown hair flowed over her feminine shoulders to the middle of her back and shined with summer highlights. She dressed in long, baggy, blue shorts, a sleeveless, white cotton blouse and flat, black shoes (but gave the impression that she would be more at home in bare feet). I derived a sensual pleasure from gazing at her from my bed, and I prolonged it as long as I could without appearing lazy or pervy.

Heidi had, for some reason, chosen not to join us, and I admitted to Judith that, although I was sure that Heidi was a wonderful girl, I was rather glad. I chose to take her to an elegant oak and-brassy type tavern which I had visited twice or thrice and, although I knew that I would end up spending at least a quarter of my remaining cash, I felt that the pleasure-per-dollar ratio would justify it.

We took a hidden corner table and began to get to know one another. I was utterly charmed and fascinated by her, and the conversation galloped along under its own power. I was amazed when, sometime later, our waiter informed us that it was nearly midnight and that they would soon be closing.

Time had slipped past us undetected and neither of us felt that our night was finished. At her suggestion, we picked up a cask of wine at the hostel and took it down to the beach, where we sat in the sand and drank facing the choppy surf. There was a warmth on the breeze which seemed to be emanating from the nearly full moon, suspended above the waves. I wasn't at all surprised when Judith kicked her shoes off, but was taken aback when she stood and began to unbutton her flimsy blouse.

"I'm going in for a swim," she declared. "Are you coming? The blouse was off. She began to unbutton her shorts.

"I don't know," I heard myself utter, "I'm not much of a water person." This was true. I've always been scared of swimming in the ocean for a couple of reasons; primarily because I swim like a rock and also because I'm terrified of sharks. They say that the odds of being eaten by a shark are about the same as being hit by lightning. Those are slim odds, sure, but I enjoy my position at the top of the food chain far too much to fuck around.

Combined with my general fear was the fact that the beaches of Australia are a favorite hangout for the infamous

Great White and the knowledge that he comes in close to shore at night to feed. I remained sitting on the sand. Judith had just removed her panties and was standing in front of me in the moonlight.

"Are you afraid?" she asked, completely free of modesty.

"Yes," I said, nodding.

"Of me or the water?"

"Of sharks."

"Oh, that's adorable," she said, as though I were a little boy. "Well, I'm going in alone then; don't you go anywhere and leave me." She turned and jogged confidently toward the breakers. I sat feeling like a complete asshole, watching the lovely, naked Judith wade into the sea, when a familiar little voice spoke in my head.

"Dave?"

"Yeah, what do you want?"

"I want to ask you a question."

"What is it?"

"I know I've been laying low these days and that I may have missed something. Just tell me one thing: Are you a gay man?"

"No..."

"'Cause if you are, I want out."

"I'm just afraid that there are sharks out there."

"You think there may be sharks out there?"

"Yes"

"And you let a girl go out there anyway?"

"Well, I..."

"Boy, you're a chivalrous bastard, aren't you Dave?"

"I just thought..."

"Did you happen to notice that she was naked?"

"Of course."

"Yet, because of the possible, yet unlikely, presence of a fish, you let a beautiful, naked girl go out there without you,

even after she asked you to go with her. And she's naked. I
understand. It makes perfect sense now..."

"Shut up! I'll go. I'm scared out of my mind, but I'll go."

"Good. Now take off your clothes, she's waiting for you. "

I stepped out of my clothes and walked toward the water
as an unseen orchestra played the theme from "Jaws" somewhere behind me. My legs were stiff with terror. I was wishing
that I hadn't removed my underwear because I had a strange
feeling that if a big Great White didn't chomp me in half, then
a small, frustrated one would sneak up and bite my pecker
off.

Adding to my great discomfort was the fact that the water
was shockingly cold, and, as I waded in, I wondered how the
hell I had talked myself into this. In the moonlight, I could see
that Judith had made it beyond the white water to the point
where she could relax and ride with the rise and fall of the
swells, and she watched me as I struggled through the surf
with all the grace and buoyancy of a man in armor. My stroke
could best be described as a half frog-paddle, because I
cupped my vulnerable privates (or are they my private vul-
nerables?) with one hand and groped through the water with
the other.

When I found myself sinking from exhaustion, I would
switch hands and inch along again. I was worn out by the
time I made it to the smiling Judith.

"I thought you were afraid of sharks," she said, bobbing
effortlessly.

"I'd rather not discuss them out here, if you don't mind," I
said, struggling to keep my head above water.

"You were very brave to swim out here," she said.

"No I wasn't. I'm scared stiff."

I then noticed that Judith was moving toward me and she
didn't stop until her face was only inches from mine.

"I find it very attractive when a man can admit that he's afraid."

"Really?"

"Yes, exceedingly."

"Well, then I'll have you know that I'm absolutely terrified."

"Stop it," she said, moving even closer, "you're driving me mad."

I pulled her gently against me and tried to kiss her, but I was shivering violently and bit her lower lip instead.

"I'm a much better kisser on dry land," I said.

"Well then perhaps we should be heading in," she suggested.

Our differences in swimming style became even more apparent as we made our way back toward shore. Just before a big wave would crash down on us from the rear, Judith would slip beneath the surface like a mermaid and reappear twenty yards further in with her glossy hair slicked back against her head. I, however, was at the mercy of every wave and was a text book example of the "Washing Machine" method of body surfing. I was thrashed and hurled toward the beach like a water-soaked towel.

Our shore landings were also markedly different; Judith glided in gracefully and landed on her feet, while I was washed up onto the sand on my back, wrapped in seaweed. As I stood and untangled myself, I looked down and saw to my horror that my penis was gone. I shrieked and turned toward the moon to shed more light on my front side and saw, to my great relief, that it was not gone but merely shriveled due to the cold and was hiding within my pubic hair. Then I noticed that Judith was looking at me.

"It's usually a lot bigger than that," I insisted.

"Oh, don't be silly, size doesn't matter." Painful words. The phrase "size doesn't matter" was coined originally by the unfulfilled, yet dutiful, female partner of a man possessing a small penis, and has been used throughout the ages by women wishing to lift the spirits of men suffering from the same congenital, genital deficiency. It was my great and urgent desire to assure Judith that the cocktail weenie which was now in my possession did not belong to me, but to some little shrively guy who had somehow switched with me and run off carrying mine over his shoulder. But, instead, I chose to remain silent on the issue and let my body speak for itself. I took her by the hand and led her back over to our spot between two small dunes, and we stood facing each other.

"There's something I don't understand," I said. "You went out of your way to tell me that you have a boyfriend. Was that true?"

"Yes, I do have a boyfriend."

"Oh. But you're standing naked here with me and I'm about to put my arms around you and kiss you."

"I hope so."

"Are you comfortable with that?" I asked.

"Completely. Before I left home, he and I talked about it and we decided that a year is an awfully long time and that we're both adults. I don't expect him to be a saint for a year and he doesn't expect me to be one either."

"I feel much better now."

"Good. Does that mean that you're going to put your arms around me and kiss me like you said you would?"

I, once again, pulled Judith gently against me and we kissed, very softly at first, but it quickly grew in intensity as we unleashed our mutual passion. She was soft and warm and lovely in my arms ... and my body began to speak for itself.

I awoke the next morning with Judith in my thoughts and sand in every orifice. Upon opening my eyes, I lay motionless for perhaps twenty minutes on my gritty sheets and replayed the previous night's beach scene over and over in my mind.

When I finally sat up, I discovered a note taped on my upper thigh. I grinned and pulled it off.

"My darling David, It's a splendid day! Heidi and I have gone to the beach. We'll be basking on a nice little spot between two dunes (I believe you know it). Please join us if you like. Otherwise, sleep all afternoon if you care to, because you won't be leaving today. Don't bother arguing, I've already paid your rent for tonight and tomorrow night. I'll see you soon. Last night was wonderful. (a very sandy) Jude"

People change, but not nearly as easily as plans do. Five days after I was supposed to be hitch-hiking north, I was still in Surfer's Paradise. In fact, I was sharing a one bedroom "flat" with Judith and Heidi. I had decided to extend my stay and spend Christmas with Judith when she and Heidi had moved into the apartment and offered me the couch. This change in plans called for a change in strategy. I was down to my last few dollars and I needed to find a way to make some money. I put on my best shirt and began wandering around town asking for work.

One of the many places I visited was a body shop (called a "panel beater" on that side of the equator), and the owner offered me a job. On the following afternoon, I began taking cars apart for ten dollars an hour. Easy money. I would earn it, however, when it came time to putting these cars back together.

Life in the flat was never dull. Judith and Heidi were both very immodest, down to earth types, and they often strode around the living room wearing nothing at all. I enjoyed these moments. They were also fine hostesses and held many cheap wine parties with international guest lists. Even Lorie the Tasmanian was invited once or twice (after vowing not to break wind). These were culturally enriching times which made me feel as though I was accomplishing something while enjoying myself immensely.

My relationship with Judith remained at, but never sur-
passed, the level of intensity that we had achieved on the
beach. I do not refer to it as a "love affair" because we did
not fall in love. I believe that we both consciously governed
our emotions and feelings for one another because we were
aware that our days together were numbered and we simply
did not allow the love to blossom.

Also, there was her boyfriend at home. When Judith
would receive a letter from him, she would disappear into her
room for a while to read it and then re-emerge as his for the
rest of the afternoon. I must admit that this was difficult for
me to accept on occasion, but she was honest with me, and
I with her, and this was just one of the cold realities of our
temporary relationship. Had the circumstances been different, things would have almost certainly escalated.

But for where we were and what we both had planned,
the times we shared were perfect.

SIX

<u>Sand in My Eggnog</u>

I f I were a permanent resident of the southern hemisphere, I would have complained long ago and attempted to start a movement to change the date of Christmas Day down under. It's easy for those in the northern hemisphere to forget, as we are decorating our trees in mid-winter and entertaining hopes of a white, Bing Crosby Christmas, that down under it's the peak of their summer and is sweltering hot. If Jesus was really as nice a guy as everybody says he was, then I'm sure he wouldn't have minded if those down south celebrated his birthday in June instead of December.

Somehow, though, many of the Christmas traditions of the north are able to permeate the heat barrier at the equator; on Christmas morning in Surfer's Paradise, a large group of us frolicked in the summer wonderland, making sand men and sand angels on the beach and being careful to avoid the eyes as we held cheery sand-ball fights. Bare-chested Santas dotted the shore in cut-off red trousers, drooping white beards, and golden tans-- the likes of which never seen around the North Pole.

To our great delight, Paul from the Backpackers United had invited us to attend Christmas dinner at the hostel. We arrived a bit early to help prepare and were impressed to see that a very long banquet table had been set up next to the pool and was set for thirty people. Though no two plates appeared to be the same, and the silverware was of all different sizes, it was about the finest arrangement I had ever seen and I was proud to have been invited.

At two o'clock the guests began to congregate as wonderful smells of Christmas emanated from the common kitchen. Lorie, looking quite dapper dressed in his Christmas best and with his beard brushed into an impressive, billowy, black mane, pulled me aside to tell me that, in honor of this grand occasion, he had been stock-piling gas and had not passed any for six days. His plan was to wait for the right moment and then give everybody the "gift of gas." I tried to talk him out of it, but the best I could do was make him promise to wait until everybody had finished eating.

When it came time to sit down, we waited until Lorie had taken his seat before Judith, Heidi and I chose our spot at the opposite end of the long table. Paul's wife, Carmen, had asked me to assist with the distribution of dinner, so, with the help of two or three others, we collected the plates in an orderly fashion, filled them with hot food in the kitchen, and then re-allocated them to the eager guests.

The fare consisted of ham, turkey, pumpkin, peas, and plumb pudding. When everybody was seated with their dinner in front of them, I heard grace of some sort spoken in no less than six languages (not including the Australian wise guy who said "two, four, six, eight, thank you God, the grub looks great").

Christmas had always been very important to me; not for religious reasons, but for the closeness it made me feel with my family. This particular Christmas was certainly different, but somehow just as meaningful. Sharing Christmas Dinner with thirty relative strangers from all over the world made me feel as though we were not really strangers after all, but, instead, friends who had never had the chance to meet. We raised our various mismatched cups and glasses and toasted in the universal language of unquestioned friendship.

All through dinner I had been keeping an eye on Lorie, wary of any warning signs. He stirred uncomfortably, his eyes darting from side to side and I knew from experience that he was preparing to go into the "death lean." He had somehow managed to situate himself between the two meek Japanese girls with whom Judith and Heidi had once shared a room, and I sincerely pitied them for the horrible shock they were about to experience. But then something completely unexpected began to develop. The girl to his left, a quiet beauty named Tomoko, seemed to be very receptive to Lorie's unique charms, and the two fell into what appeared to be heart-felt, flirtatious conversation.

Lorie was exhibiting a gentleness of which I never dreamed he was capable. He blushed and giggled and young Tomoko was absolutely captivated. I then witnessed something which was almost certainly a first for the burly Tasmanian: he stood, bowed gracefully to an impressed Tomoko, and excused himself from the table. He winked at me as he passed, and I gave him the thumbs up, for I knew exactly what he was doing.

As he walked toward his room, which was only about twenty feet from where I sat, I felt proud of Lorie for the choice he had just made. After he had entered his room and closed the door, there was a moment of silence before the rumbling began.

At the onset, the sounds emanating from behind his door were like the distant snores of a sleeping giant, but, as he relaxed his great sphincter, the tones became deeper and truer and began to sound remarkably like a novice practicing scales on the tuba. Several others at the table heard the sounds, but I was the only one who knew what was making them. They cocked their heads and offered guesses as to their origin. A New Zealander to my left said,

"It sounds like geese honking." A Swedish girl said,

"No, no. I am certain it is a horn."

"Maybe a fog horn," said a young Canadian guy.

"But there's no fog," said another Swede. I, however, knew differently. Behind the door of room #9 was a killer fog which, if released, would put a quick and revolting end to Christmas.

I had been able to save over six hundred dollars working as a panel beater and, on my last day there, the day after Christmas, good fortune placed its hand upon my shoulder. Steve, the boss, was a real wheeler-dealer and was always on the prowl for an automotive bargain. He often purchased old, beat-to-shit cars, got them running, gave them quick paint jobs and sold them at a three-hundred percent profit. Word got around that he was the man to see if you wanted to unload an old beater.

On my last afternoon at the shop, a young Canadian traveler pulled up and in an old, dilapidated station wagon and asked Steve if he wanted to buy it for four hundred dollars. Steve offered him a hundred, and the obviously desperate Canadian reluctantly accepted.

Steve was well aware of my financial situation and knew, also, that I planned to leave town the following day and hitchhike up the coast. He asked me if I would rather drive my own car. This was a classic example of being in the right place at the right time, and he sold me the old wagon for $150. I was ecstatic.

The make of my new car was Holden, and it had been assembled in an Australian factory in the year 1968, when I was six years old and just learning my first dirty words. It had been a blue car in its glory days, and still was, technically, but, over the decades, it had aged into a faded, sunbaked-memory-of-blue. She was not "smashed up" — there were no large dents or holes in her body and her overall shape was intact. However, she was literally covered, from bumper to bumper, with little dings and blemishes which, when combined with the washed-out blue, made the car look blurry.

Until I became used to it, I would blink and rub my eyes when I'd look at her from a distance because she seemed out of focus. But the old car possessed a quality which made her look absolutely beautiful to me, and that was the fact that she was mine. I had the title in my pocket, and she was the finest set of wheels I had ever seen. The old Holden represented my access to Australia.

Saying good-bye to Judith was quite sad for me because I knew I'd never see her again. Even though I'd known all along that we had no future together, walking away from her was very difficult. This was my first real brush with the "dark side" of travel. The joy and excitement of meeting people and forming new relationships is balanced by the sadness and letdown of saying good-bye. I kissed Judith one last time and left her in her flat. My spirits were low, and I did my best to view our separation as a growing experience which would help build my character by forcing me to accept inevitable change.

I couldn't leave town without stopping by the hostel to say "so long" to all those with whom I had shared so much wine and good fun. Most of those I had come to know well had moved on, but a few remained. I also wanted to show off my new wheels. There were a few who laughed at my station wagon, but, to the average backpacker, a car is an unaffordable luxury and most of them envied me for my good fortune. I knocked before entering Lorie's open door and was pleased to see the Lovely Tomoko sitting on his knee and trimming Lorie's beard.

"I never thought I'd see the day when you'd break down and trim that shrub," I said.

"Anything to please the little lady, mate. I've even given up farting... well, I haven't actually given up, I just take walks by myself."

"This must be serious."

"Oh, it is, Yank. You're looking at the mother of my children." (An image of a bunch of little Asian kids with big, fluffy beards running around the house flashed in my mind and I smiled).

"I'm happy for you Lorie; and you, too, Tomoko."

"Lawrence is a beautiful man," she said, and pulled off Lorie's hat to begin trimming his hair. This was the first time I had never seen him without a hat on, and I was quite surprised to see the baldest, whitest, shiniest scalp I had ever seen.

"Didn't know I was bare on top, did ya mate?" Tomoko began to brush his horseshoe crown of hair, which, like trees on a mountain, did not grow above a certain elevation,

"No, I never knew," I said. "You look very dignified."

"Lawrence has a beautiful head," boasted Tomoko.

"Yes, it's a very nice head," I agreed. "Well, Lorie, I'm on my way north. I bought myself an old car."

"What sort of car did you get?" he asked.

"It's a 1968 Holden HK station wagon," I said, proudly.

"Is she running alright?"

"Yeah, she runs great." (This was mostly true. Everything but the brakes seemed to be fine).

"Yank, that's a fine machine. If you just keep her full of oil and petrol, she'll take you right 'round Australia if you ask her to."

"That's what I want to hear," I said, "because that's exactly what I plan to do." Since so many travelers had come and gone at the hostel and I was on my way out of town anyway, I had been paying no attention to the stranger who was lying on his corner bunk, reading.

"Pardon me," he said, sitting up, "I'm Andrew from Scotland. I couldn't help but overhear that you're driving north in your new car. Would you consider having me along? I'll pay for half the petrol and I have an honors degree in engineering, so if anything goes wrong with the old girl, I can direct you in your repairs."

I liked Andrew instantly. He was very pompous. Fifteen minutes after I had met him, he was loading his luggage into the back of the station wagon. He did not own a backpack, but two fine leather cases and a matching suit carrier.

"Do you drink beer?" I asked him.

"Profusely," he answered.

"Then I guess we should get some for the road."

"That's a fine idea," he said, "Would you allow me to pay for the first lot?"

I felt that Andrew and I were going to get along just fine.

SEVEN

The Road North

As we pulled out of Surfer's Paradise, the earth began to revolve again. My feeling was that I had stayed in Surfer's Paradise far too long and I was hungry to get some miles under my bald tires.

I had been in the country for over a month, but I felt that I had not yet seen the true face of Australia. On the other hand, had I left sooner, I probably would not have gotten together with the lovely, unforgettable Judith; and I certainly would have missed the opportunity of acquiring my own car.

Christmas had also been an experience I would never forget and I had twenty new names in my address book, which was quickly developing into an international mailing list of colorful characters. And next to me on the bench seat was my newest friend, Andrew, who, thirty minutes earlier, I had never met. We cracked our first beer on the way out of town and I began to get to know the young Scot who was going to see Australia with me.

McInnes. Andrew Cameron McInnes. Well-bred and educated, he reminded me of a young David Niven, sharing the same refinement, wit, and smooth style (a minor difference being Andrew's Scottish accent which caused his R's to roll and last a bit longer than Mr. Niven's). He was a little taller than I, about 5'11," rather slight, with brown scrunchy hair and a very aristocratic British nose which turned down slightly at the tip like the beak of an eagle. He made it abundantly clear that he wanted very much to appear dashing -- and every now and then he did exhibit a flash of dash -- but, at twenty-five, he was still too young.

One cannot be truly dashing, I felt, until one is also distinguished. There was no doubt in my mind, however, that by the time he reached thirty-five, he would be the epitome of "dashing." I could see this because Andrew had clearly decided at an early age exactly what he would be like when he was full grown and had become a young version of himself as an older man. I envied him for this quality because, as I was zigging and zagging through life, making painfully slow progress, Andrew was sailing a true course, making a bee line for his future.

His circumstances at home in Scotland which had led to his departure were completely different from those which had led to mine. He had graduated with honors from a respected university and was offered several positions right away. He chose a career with Mars, Inc., representing the candy bar maker as an account executive in Scotland, Northern England, and Ireland. His salary was substantial. His social life was charged. His future was jelling. However, he awoke one morning in a sweat and realized that his momentum was carrying him toward a life he did not want. He knew, also, that the longer he waited, the more difficult it would become to get out. His decision was to escape.

Complicating his departure plan was a girlfriend with whom he had been contemplating marriage. She was a rich, beautiful brunette with royal ties and was a star member of the British National Equestrian Team. One night at tea however, she had removed her gloves to dunk a crumpet and

Andrew noticed for the first time that all the years of horse handling had left her with masculine hands, so he no longer considered her suitable for marriage or a strong enough reason to keep him from leaving the country.

"I'm going to Australia," he told her, and two weeks later he was on a jet bound for Sydney. After spending two months in Sydney (a city he considered "a tiny oasis in a cultural desert"), Andrew arrived at the conclusion that the earliest white inhabitants of Australia -- the convicted habitual criminals who had been exiled from England -- had passed on to their descendants all of the nastiness and thuggery which had led to their exile, resulting in a barbarous populous consisting almost entirely of classless ruffians.

Though I didn't exactly agree with Andrew's view on Australians, I enjoyed his opinionated snobbishness. The only quiet moments along the road were when one of us was sleeping on the mattress in the back. The rest of the time was filled with enthusiastic conversation and laughter. The more I got to know McInnes, the more I realized that I was living in my own world of round-edged generalities. I took my surroundings for granted and merely derived as much pleasure as I could from them without questioning.

Andrew, on the other hand, took notice of the world around him, categorized, theorized, and criticized. He digested what he saw, processed whom he met and arrived at conclusions about everything. He was adamant about some subjects, yet always gracious and never angry. I had never met anyone quite as British as Andrew McInnes (although, as he often reminded, he was a pure Scot).

While I admired him for all of these qualities, Andrew claimed that he envied me for a few of mine. He said that I possessed a "rawness" and an "honest spontaneity" of which he no longer felt capable. Children exhibit these qualities, he said, but nearly everybody sheds them as they grow older.

When I explained to him that I had left America to outgrow the very boyishness he admired, he told me that if I were to do so it would be a "tragedy."

"If you can achieve the adult traits you're after," he said, "and maintain that fresh, child-like perspective, the world will be yours."

It soon became clear to both of us that he and I were perfectly balanced as a pair. We brought out the very best in one another and stood out of the crowd everywhere we stopped.

On the road between two small towns, we decided that we were worthy of a title. We were unable to agree on one, so we chose two. By day, we were the "Adventure Brothers"; we would slay any beast, permeate any impermeable jungle and basically laugh in the face of death as long as the sun was up. But as soon as the sun ducked beneath the horizon, we became "The Knights of Chivalry." As the Knights of Chivalry, we would drink very dry martinis, rescue damsels in distress and do our best to act like Sean Connery.

Eager to try out these new roles, we pulled over at a small roadside store. The sun had just gone down. We were the Knights of Chivalry. A little bell jingled as we strolled through the door, as cool and as debonair as two young men could imagine themselves as being. Behind the counter, leaning on a stool, was a very large, balding man with red eyes and a red face. He was absorbed in a smutty magazine which his eyes left reluctantly as we glided up to the counter. My chin was up; my chest and elbows were out.

"We, kind sir," I boomed triumphantly, "are the KNIGHTS OF CHIVALRY!" McInnes joined in,

"Would you happen to know the whereabouts of any fair, young maidens who may require our assistance?" He stood next to me, poised in an equally proud stance.

The big man was obviously irritated to be taken away from his "Hustler" for this, and his face showed it.

"What the hell are you on about?" he snapped, burning us with his blood-shot eyes. McInnes and I slouched simultaneously and we were just two ordinary guys again. I managed a few meek words.

"I, uh, said that we're the, you know, knights of chivalry..."

"Well why don't you get a real fucking job?!" he bellowed, glowering at us. I was speechless and utterly deflated. Somehow McInnes was able to muster the strength to buy two Mars bars, and we limped out to the car like a pair of beaten dogs. We sat for a few seconds, staring blankly out the windshield, before we began to laugh.

"Well," I said, "our debut as the Knights of Chivalry wasn't quite as earth-shaking as we'd hoped it would be, was it?" Tears ran down Andrew's cheeks as he laughed at the thought of what assholes we had just made of ourselves.

"No," he said, struggling for breath. "I don't think he was too impressed with us." I didn't want Andrew to feel as though he was my guest in the car, so I declared that, since we were partners, the car was half his. He was quite touched, particularly because the old Holden was proving to be a magic machine capable of doing whatever we asked of her. We then decided that our wonderful vehicle was worthy of a title, just like we were. This was difficult and took half a day, but we finally agreed on one. The name we chose was "Ol' Creampuff," a beautifully descriptive term I'd learned from an old car salesman with whom I'd worked long before.

We bought a can of white paint and brushed "Ol' Creampuff" on her doors and "Onward Creampuff!" on the tailgate. Our paintmanship wasn't the best, but she looked quite impressive anyway.

At the beginning of each day, when we would climb into Ol' Creampuff for the first time, whoever was driving would announce, "Secure yourself, I'm going to fire the main engine!" Of course, there was only one motor under the hood, but we enjoyed referring to it as "the main engine." She would roar into life the first try every time, and then immediately settle into a pleasant, throaty purr. The speedometer was in miles-per-hour, not kilometers, because 01' Creampuff was a relic from the days before Australia had gone metric.

Her cruising speed was seventy-two; she was capable of going much faster, but we found that she developed a disconcerting wobble at seventy-three. I mentioned once before that the brakes were less than perfect. Stopability varied, but the brakes always seemed to work fine when we needed them most. However, the most crucial piece of equipment in the car was also the simplest. Located under the dash, on the driver's side, was a small, nondescript, black box. On the two-inch square face was a silver toggle switch next to an octagonal, convex, red plastic lens, perhaps the size of a dime. An upward flip of the toggle activated the Red Light; it looked like a glowing ruby.

The Red Light was not connected to any other device on Ol' Creampuff. It was not an indicator light installed to notify the driver that the heater or the fog lamps had been activated. A flip of the switch did not turn on the radio -- there wasn't one. It was simply the Red Light, and it was infinitely more important than all of those things. The Red Light represented the magic and the soul of 01' Creampuff. We decided that we would use the Red Light only in case of emergency.

The first time we were saved by the Red Light was during a violent, midnight thunderstorm. Roughly ten hours earlier, on the previous afternoon, we had been heading north on the coastal highway, and were perhaps 50 miles south of the beach city of Mackay. McInnes was behind the wheel, cruising at seventy-two, when he spotted an old wooden sign next to the road which read "Crocodile River 37 Kilometers." A faded arrow beneath the words pointed to the west.

"What do you think, fellow Adventure Brother?" he asked. "Should we investigate Crocodile River?"

"Need you ask, fellow adventure Brother?" I replied. McInnes guided Ol' Creampuff off the highway onto a very narrow, overgrown dirt road.

One hundred feet down the road, which was really no more than a trail, was an ancient, sagging, wooden gate blocking the way. Nailed to the middle was a peeling sign which read "Road Closed." McInnes showed no sign of slowing, and he wore a crazed look.

"I think I'm going to ram it, old boy," he announced.

"Onward Creampuff!' I shouted. The old road block disintegrated on the grill and hood without slowing us down. The road beyond abruptly became even more overgrown and was difficult to distinguish from the adjacent flora. Though the road had clearly not been used for years, McInnes did a fine job of holding to it.

After nearly an hour of plowing through thick vegetation, we came to the lip of a shallow valley. Three hundred feet below us, on the valley floor, flowing right to left, was the Crocodile River; wide, brown, and slow. The remnant road wound down the steep hillside and terminated in a flat, rocky area at the river's edge. We parked facing down river, cracked a cold beer, cast our fishing lines, and began looking around for crocodiles.

Seeing no crocodiles in or along the Crocodile River was a little disappointing, but we knew that there was at least one around. Just thirty feet from Ol' Creampuff we found strange marks and tracks on the bank which could have only been made by a large crocodile. We looked around for him, but evidently, he did not want to be seen. Lucky for him, too, because McInnes had his Swiss army knife drawn and was on a quest to make matching belts and brief cases for the Knights of Chivalry.

Though our hunt for large reptiles may have been fruitless, our fishing was not and it wasn't long before we had three in the fire. There are two types of fish on this planet that I can readily identify; they are the shark and the goldfish. The three we caught were strangers to me, and to McInnes, but they tasted just fine roasted right on the coals. Complementing the mystery fish were a couple of coconuts; a lovely bunch of which we had picked along the coast and stowed in the back of Ol' Creampuff for just such occasions.

As sundown approached, we decided to make the peaceful riverside spot our campsite for the night. The strange fish, which looked sort of like a cross between a small shark and a goldfish, were certainly plentiful, and we just couldn't think of any reason to leave yet. We'd spent much of the day in the potent summer sun, and the direct rays, along with the few beers we'd had, had sapped us of our energy. I unzipped my sleeping bag and laid it out at the water's edge, while McInnes climbed onto the mattress in the back of Ol' Creampuff for his nap.

Just as I was beginning to doze, the first raindrop fell on my cheek. We had gotten used to the sporadic Summer showers, so I thought nothing of it. I picked up my sleeping bag and continued my nap lying across the front seat of the car. It must have been four hours later when I was awakened by a violent thunderclap. I snapped upright, completely disoriented and another thunderclap exploded, seemingly right on top of Ol' Creampuff. Lightning glowed through the translucent, fogged-up windows and, in the half-second of luminescence, I saw that McInnes was sitting up in the back, rubbing his eyes.

"What's all the racket, old boy?"

"It's a thunderstorm," I said.

"Have you spotted any young maidens who may require our assistance?"

"Not one."

"Then I'm going back to sleep," he said, and fell back into the darkness.

I rolled down the passenger-side window to look out at the interesting weather and I noted that the river was running past at a much faster rate than it had been earlier. Panic suddenly engulfed me like a wave when I realized that, the last time I had looked, the passenger side had been facing away from the river. I bolted across the bench seat and rolled the driver's window down. The sight of the black water racing past sickened me.

"McInnes! Wake up! We're in the river!" Thunder exploded again as the sky short circuited in a series of white-blue flashes; the pounding of the rain on the roof increased in intensity and the noise was deafening. I shot back across the seat, opened the passenger's door, and stepped out. The water came up to the middle of my calf, and was just an inch short of flowing into the car. The sky lit up again for half-an-instant and I saw exactly what was happening. The Mighty Crocodile had jumped its banks and we were on the verge of being swallowed by the river and swept away.

As I slid behind the wheel, McInnes appeared next to me in the passenger seat.

"What seems to be the problem?" he asked.

"The river's jumped its banks; we've got to get the hell out of here! Are you ready?"

"Ready, old boy," he replied.

"Secure yourself," I shouted. "I'm going to fire the main engine!" Ol' Creampuff roared into life. It is important to note at this point that she was equipped with only one windshield wiper, and it was on the passenger side. It had become almost automatic for Andrew and me to respond to an unexpected rain shower by the passenger reaching across and

manning the wheel, leaving the "driver" to operate the ped-
als. I turned on the headlights and the windshield wiper and
I felt McInnes take hold of the wheel.

I could see nothing through the water blasting against my
side of the windshield. I pulled the gear lever back into
"drive."

"Give her one-third power!" commanded McInnes. "We've
got to try and make it up the hill!"

I stepped on the gas, and the car began to shake.

"One third power!" he yelled.

"It is! I am! The wheels are spinning!"

"One half power!" he hollered.

I increased throttle to fifty percent, yet we still did not
move. I realized suddenly that my feet were getting very cold,
and when I reached down, I discovered at least three inches
of water on the floor.

"We're filling up with water!" I yelled. "I'm taking her up to
full power!"

Ol' Creampuff shook violently as I pushed the pedal to the
floor. The rear end bounced and danced slightly, but the
wheels continued to spin in the muddy water. I let up on the
gas momentarily to avoid sinking the rear tires and I put my
head out the window to assess our situation. As I squinted to
see up-river through the darkness and the rain, thunder
shook the car and it was daylight for an instant. During that
brief moment, I saw a three-dimensional snapshot of a nightmare. Perhaps one hundred yards up-river, moving toward
us with great velocity and rumbling like the sea, was a four-
foot wall of water stretching from bank to bank and beyond.

"Holy shit!" I screamed. "There's a giant wave coming! It's
time to turn on the Red Light!"

"Is this an emergency?" asked McInnes. Without responding, I reached under the dash and groped for the switch. I

could sense the approach of the massive wave and I knew that we were only two or three seconds from impact.

My frustration turned to fury as the toggle evaded my frantic fingers. Giving up, I placed both hands on the wheel to brace myself for the great force which was about to slam into us from the rear. McInnes had not given up, however and, suddenly, the Red Light flickered into life, glowing like an ember and dimly illuminating the inside of the car. Andrew's eyes locked with mine in the pink glow and I stomped on the accelerator.

"Onward Creampuff!" we yelled together. As the rear tires bit into the river bottom, the great wall of water crashed into the back of Ol' Creampuff launching us forward with such force that our heads snapped back. We were carried along the bank of the Mighty Crocodile for nearly twenty feet before McInnes cranked the wheel to the left. The front tires found the bottom and we shot up the bank and out of the water at forty miles an hour. I could see nothing ahead of us, but I kept the pedal to the floor.

"Keep it at full power!" screamed McInnes. "We're going up the hill!" We fish-tailed and bounced violently as we began our ascent. Being careful to keep the accelerator pressed to the floor, I leaned out my open window to get a look at the terrain ahead.

The ancient dirt road had, itself, become a river, and a foot of muddy, gravel-filled water blasted head-on into the face of Ol' Creampuff. But she never slowed. Her incredibly powerful main engine fired us up and over the top of the ridge and to safety. I let up on the gas, reached down under the dash, and turned off the Red Light.

EIGHT

The Coast

McInnes and I were certainly in no great hurry as we meandered up the east coast of Australia. The combination of having a car and absolutely no short-term time limitations or obligations gave us a freedom and an overall comfort of living that was euphoric.

Anything of interest in the periphery was investigated and utilized as fuel for the furnace of our good time. We met and overcame countless challenges as The Adventure Brothers and charmed many a damsel as The Knights of Chivalry. Ol" Creampuff carried us through jungles, across rivers and over mountains and the way we were living was probably as close to a true adventure as I'll ever come.

After six weeks on and off the road, we had put almost three thousand miles on Ol' Creampuff's odometer, yet travelled a linear distance of only 800. It was the fifteenth day of February when we pulled into the town of Airlie Beach. Before investigating the town itself, we headed straight down to the water to check out the level of the tide.

We had gotten into the habit of watching the tides because, when the sea withdrew, she exposed the rocks and the reefs which were home to the inconspicuous oyster. Not everybody cares for raw oysters. I happened to love them and so did McInnes. For this reason, we were delighted to see an extremely low tide off of Airlie Beach. Armed with screw drivers, we wandered out onto the jagged rocks and began scouring them for our favorite shellfish.

Two hours later, we sat bloody-knuckled and smiling on a picnic bench on the beach, feasting on fresh oysters and washing them down with equally fresh coconut water (we also had a jar of horseradish we carried with us for the oysters). This was a meal we had become accustomed to, yet we never tired of it. And, of course, we developed our preferences.

The oysters, we found, were best when rinsed with fresh water, because when eaten straight from the rock, the residual seawater made them too salty. The coconuts were best when green, both for the water and the meat. They could be stored for very long periods, but the older and browner they became, the tougher the meat. The meal of oysters and coconuts was one which required a substantial amount of work to put on the table. Finding and recognizing the oysters was difficult enough; prying them off the rocks was quite a task, too. Then they had to be shucked.

And, although the beaches were often littered with coconuts, the best ones were usually still high in the palms (I recall an instance when McInnes was at least twenty feet up, clinging precariously to the trunk of a palm with one arm, and swinging a stick at a stubborn coconut with the other.

"Why couldn't Mother Nature have been a little more cooperative and put coconuts on bushes?" he yelled down to me). And husking a green coconut would take us as long as half an hour. But all the labor made the meal taste that much better and, besides, we were the Adventure Brothers and we had this image of ourselves to which we constantly had to live up.

After finishing our seaside lunch, we walked into town to check things out. Airlie Beach was everything that Surfer's Paradise was not; no high-rise hotels or shopping malls; no loudspeakers spewing commercials over the beach; no pedicabs or hotdog stands littering the corners.

This was a small, quiet, one-road beach community which tolerated a slow trickle of tourists and did just fine with or without them. And, while most of Surfer's Paradise had been owned by the Japanese, Airlie Beach was strictly Australian.

The waters along the shore were emerald green and completely flat (definitely the most inviting I had ever seen, yet unsafe to enter without the protection of a full wet suit due to the seasonal presence of great numbers of the deadly Box Jellyfish, known locally as "stingers"). The lack of waves was due to the presence of the Great Barrier Reef, fifty miles offshore. And between the reef and the shore, were the more than seventy Whitsunday Islands which dotted the horizon.

For the past week, McInnes and I had been discussing the prospect of stopping and settling some place for a while. Our reservoir of funds had dwindled to a puddle and after a month and a half of living out of Ol' Creampuff, stopping for a while seemed like a very attractive idea. After fifteen minutes in Airlie Beach, we decided that we wouldn't find a nicer place to settle. We then began making inquiries as to the availability of budget accommodation and we were directed to the local Backpackers.

Located at the north end of town, "#13 Begley" was unexpectedly luxurious for a hostel. Designed and built originally as a condominium development, it sat in six separate tiers on a hill facing the sea, offering panoramic views from almost every room, and boasting a Jacuzzi on every level. For some reason, the condo's did not sell; the bank foreclosed, and the property ended up in the hands of an entrepreneur with different plans. We learned all of this information from the pretty receptionist who was obviously born without a blabbus (the gland in the base of the brain which automatically silences a person when they've said enough).

To conserve funds, McInnes and I decided that only one of us would sleep in the hostel each night and the other on the mattress in the back of 01' Creampuff and we would alternate nightly. We paid the talkative receptionist for five nights in advance, crashed out for a couple of hours (a "heads" on a coin toss had given me the bunk for the first night) and walked into town to spend the last of our money on beer.

I awoke the next morning with a beautiful Swedish contortionist named Eva sharing my sheets. We had met over a pitcher of beer, and, two hours later, she had grabbed me by the hair and said "Take me to your bed now or lose me forever." Apparently she had been sending me signals which I had been failing to receive (which was very unlike me. I was far more likely to imagine non-existent sexual advances than I was to overlook legitimate ones).

Her travelling companion, Polly, a very exotic looking girl from the West Indies, had taken a liking to McInnes and spent the night with him in the back of 01' Creampuff. These two were great fun and we asked them if they'd like to accompany us on our trek around the continent, but they were heading in the opposite direction and had to decline. I was disappointed because I liked Eva. McInnes was disappointed, too, because he liked Polly.

At noon, the girls were gone and we were broke. I spotted a 3x5 card on the hostel bulletin board which read "Experienced Gardener Wanted -- Eight Dollars per Hour." Five minutes later I dialed the number and a man answered.

"Hello," I began, "I found the card here at the hostel which says that you're looking for a gardener."

"Yes, I am. You sound American."

"I am American."

"How long will you be in Airlie Beach?"

"Oh, several months," I lied.

"Do you have much experience in gardening and land-scaping?"

"Oh, yes, I've gardened and landscaped quite a bit at home in America."

"Have you ever done it professionally?"

"Oh, yes, very professionally." (I always began a sentence with "oh" if I was planning to lie).

"Do you mind waking up early?" he asked.

"Oh, no." McInnes dropped me off at eight the next morning and headed off to the local employment office to find a job of his own. He could afford to be a little more selective than I in his job hunting because, like Scotland, Australia is a member of the British Commonwealth and he was entitled to work there legally. I, on the other hand, was breaking the law by working and was forced to accept menial jobs where I could maintain my anonymity and be paid "under the table."

I knocked on the front door and met the man to whom I had spoken on the phone. He struck me as a pretty decent guy as he walked me around his property to show me what he expected of me as his gardener. Picture a large, two-story home built on a hill in a dense rain forest. My new mission in life was to reclaim the two acres on which this man's house was built from the ever-advancing rain forest which was threatening from all sides.

"Well, Mr. Hopwood," I began, "this is certainly a big job, but no bigger than any gardening or landscaping jobs I tackled back in America. The only problem is, I've never worked for anything less than twelve dollars an hour."

"You made twelve dollars an hour as a gardener in America?"

"Oh, yes, as a minimum."

"Well, the most I can possibly pay you is ten." The trouble with lying about work experience is that there will come a time when one has to prove oneself. I had put a great deal of pressure on myself by requesting and receiving a two dollar per hour raise before I'd even started, but I was determined to be the best damn American gardener in Airlie Beach.

At three that afternoon I stood sweating, panting, and itching on top of the five-foot wall which ran up the hill alongside Mr. Hopwood's driveway. A few seconds earlier, I had been at the bottom of the hill, hacking at foliage and swatting mosquitoes, when I nearly tripped over a rotten log. Being the thorough landscaper that I was, I began attempting to remove the pesky eyesore.

As I lifted one end of the log, I discovered, to my surprise, a three-foot goanna lizard hiding underneath. I probably would have run away anyway, but this damn lizard hissed at me and whipped me on the leg with his tail. I screamed, ran up the hill in fast motion, and sprang up on top of the wall. The giant lizard was nowhere in sight. I then heard a sliding door open onto the balcony above and I looked up to see Mr. Hopwood staring down at me.

"Was that a scream I just heard, mate?"

"Oh, no. I breathed in a bug and I was trying to get it back out."

"Well, your mate's on the phone. He wants to talk to you." He lowered the receiver down to me by the cord. It was McInnes on the phone, of course.

"Hello, old boy. How's the new career working out?" I didn't want to let him know that my entire body itched, my back ached, I had bleeding blisters on my hands and I had just been chased up the hill by a three-foot lizard.

"Oh, great," I lied.

"Glad to hear it. Hey, I've got a job, too."

"You sound a bit fuzzy," I said. "Where are you?"

"Sorry about that," he said, "I'm on a cellular phone. You wouldn't believe where I am right now. I went to the employment office and it just so happened that they were looking for someone to start right away. I'm here on Hamilton Island. They paid for the ferry ride over and I started this morning."

"You're on Hamilton Island?"

"Yes. It's absolutely beautiful here."

"And what is it you're doing out on Hamilton Island?"

"I'm a water-skiing instructor. We've finished for the day, so I'm lying on the beach having a mai-tai with Mimi."

"Who's 'Mimi'?" I asked, not really wanting to know the answer.

"Mimi is a co-worker. She also models bikinis for the guests, although she's only wearing half of her suit right now. Would you care to say hello to Mimi?" I could clearly hear Mimi giggling in the background. She sounded very pretty.

"No thanks." I didn't feel like talking to Mimi. At that moment, I looked down and noticed a giant green ant on the back of my hand. I knew he was going to bite me, because that was how my day was going, but this foreknowledge didn't make it hurt any less. I screamed again, lost my balance, fell off the wall and rolled halfway down the hill. Mr. Hopwood, who had witnessed the incident, hauled the phone back up by the cord.

"Are you alright, Mulligan?"

"I'm okay," I said from inside the prickly bush I had rolled into. Mr. Hopwood then spoke into the phone, no doubt telling McInnes what had happened. He hung up after a few seconds.

"Your mate asked me to tell you that Creampuff is at the hostel, and that he'll be back to visit when he's able." Until that moment, I had never harbored any ill feelings for McInnes. As I emerged from the prickly bush and brushed the dirt and bugs off of my body, I imagined McInnes lying on the beach next to Mimi, drinking his mai-tai and talking on his cellular phone. I then saw myself, with delightful clarity, swinging him around by his neck and opening a coconut with his head.

Over the next four weeks I accomplished something which was a first for me. I concentrated all of my efforts and focused all of my attention on my job. While I had entered the role of gardener reluctantly, viewing it as a menial, demeaning position, I soon became proud of the progress I was making on Mr. Hopwood's property. Mr. Hopwood, too, was very pleased with my performance and even told me that I was well worth the ten dollars an hour he was paying me. This was the first time ever in my life that an employer of mine had expressed great delight in having hired me. In every job I'd ever held, I'd done well to start with, but soon lost interest and ended up in a vegetative state where I would simply go through the motions for a period before quitting.

At the end of one month of gardening in Airlie Beach, I had landscaped everything there was to landscape on Mr. Hopwood's property and my job was completed. He paid me my last week's wages, thanked me for all the hard work and shook my hand.

I walked away, chin up, from a job well done.

The Death of a Legend

My final responsibility to Mr. Hopwood was to return the gas-powered weed trimmer to the store where he had rented it. I tossed it in the back of 01' Creampuff, drove the fifteen miles over the hill to the town of Canonvale where the store was located and returned the rented defoliator without incident.

Heading back towards home, I had to, once again, drive over the high, steep hill which separated Canonvale from Airlie Beach. I had driven the coastal road countless times since arriving in Airlie. It flattened out at the summit for roughly fifty yards, then curved slightly before sloping down the other side. Ol' Creampuff hummed her velvety purr as she carried me up the steep grade and I eased up slightly on the gas as we achieved the summit.

Ahead, where the road began to curve to the right, was a road block which I had passed on my way out of Airlie Beach. An orange-vested road crew was filling pot holes and hand-painting a yellow line and perhaps half a dozen cars were stopped and waiting to proceed ahead of me in my lane (which was on the left, remember). Traffic in the oncoming lane was being allowed through and, judging by the number of cars zipping by in the opposite direction, they had been held up for a while. I was travelling at approximately thirty-five miles an hour when I applied the brakes to stop for the road block. Nothing happened. The pedal went directly to the floor without offering any resistance.

I began to frantically pump the pedal in an attempt to acquire some pressure, but none developed. Since Ol' Creampuff wasn't equipped with an emergency brake, my next move was to try and throw the gear lever into park. I shoved the handle forward as hard as I could, but it wouldn't move past neutral. I had less than three seconds to make my next decision.

I had two choices: I could either ram into the rear of the stationary car ahead of me, or I could veer to the left, go outside the guard rail and do my best to avoid going over the edge of the cliff. As I rapidly approached the car ahead of me, I caught the gaze of the woman driver in her rear-view mirror. I could tell by the size of her eyes that she knew I was out of control and she was preparing for impact. At the last possible moment, I turned the wheel to the left, shot across the three-foot dirt shoulder and just made it around the guard rail at the beginning of the curve. I then steered to the right, attempting to stay along the outside of the guard rail and hug the top of the hill until I could slow.

What I had been unable to see from the road, however, was a six-foot round boulder protruding from the earth around the bend. I slammed into it at thirty miles an hour and came to a very abrupt stop. My inertia upon impact carried the car a few feet to the left and 01' Creampuff was teetering on the edge of disaster.

The grassy area outside the guard rail where I had intended to make my escape was roughly six feet wide. It was almost level adjacent to the rail, but became progressively steeper until dropping off completely at cliff's edge. One hundred feet below were the rocks and the sea.

Somehow, Ol' Creampuff clung to the cliff's edge at an impossible angle and I gripped the steering wheel to keep from sliding across the seat and falling out the passenger window. I couldn't understand what was holding us to the hill; I was no physicist, but I could see and feel by our angle that we should have flipped over the edge. Then I looked down and saw that the Red Light was on. Perhaps the impact had flipped the switch. Perhaps I had kicked it. Perhaps.

Good Ol" Creampuff suddenly let out a great metallic moan, like the anguished cry of a sinking, dying ship and it began to dawn on me that she was just holding on so that I might escape. Being careful to avoid disturbing our delicate, unnatural balance, I slowly began hoisting myself up and out of the driver's side window. When my head and shoulders emerged, I saw that several people had left their cars and were rushing over to gawk at me in my predicament.

Just as I lifted my right knee out of the window and placed my foot on the outside of the door (ironically, right on the "C" in 01' Creampuff's painted name), she sighed another fatigued-steel complaint and the uphill tires lifted slowly away from the grass. Being in or on a large automobile which is in the process of turning over causes a nauseating loss of security. A car is meant to roll along, not over, and when it happens, the earth tilts on its axis and life's equilibrium is scrambled.

As we swept slowly past perpendicular, I was able to get my other foot out and onto the door and I sprang clear of my dying companion. I landed softly on my feet on the wild grass, turned and saw Ol' Creampuff's exposed belly as she quietly disappeared over the edge.

During the forty-five minute ferry ride over to Hamilton Island, I thought about how I would break the news of Ol'

Creampuff's demise to McInnes. I would tell him of the way the Red Light had mysteriously turned on by itself, how she had held on to the cliff top just long enough for me to escape and how I had climbed down to where her broken body lay on the on the rocks just in time to see the Red Light fade to a dim glow, flash brilliantly for an instant and then go black forever. The news would sadden him, I was sure, but I knew that he would emphasize the positive, like always, and say something like, "It's a shame the old girl had to go, but it sounds as though she went valiantly."

Before I'd boarded the big ferry bound for the world-class island resort, I took eight hundred dollars I'd saved as a gardener and hid it under a big rock. It seemed a comfortably suitable place to put it; perhaps because of the way I'd earned it. I thought about putting the money in a bank, but this idea quickly passed and I stashed the wad under the rock. This left me with two hundred bucks in my pocket to spend on the island.

McInnes had told me a little bit about the island over the phone, but I still wasn't prepared for what I saw when we chugged slowly into the protected marina. Money. Big dollars. There was row after row of yachts; mostly sailing vessels, but many power cruisers too. Handsome people holding cocktails dotted the decks. Everywhere I looked were dark tans and white teeth.

Music drifted on the breeze, along with perfumes, smoke, Tanqueray and laughter. I knew right away that this was a very good place to be, but, at the same time, I felt a little like I was crashing a black-tie party in a pair of overalls. I became paranoid for a moment and just knew that someone was going to point at me and shout "Hey, that guy's a gardener and he's only got two hundred dollars with him!" I began to wish that I hadn't left so much of my money back under the rock.

When the big ferry eased up alongside the dock, a couple of striped deck hands got busy and secured us with heavy rope and the body of passengers began to trickle down the gang plank in single file. I remained on the top deck because I had not yet spotted McInnes among those waiting on the dock, and I didn't wish to give him the upper hand in our re-union by allowing him to see me first. I knew he was hovering somewhere close by, but he would consider it too conven-tional and predictable to merely wait for me among the rest of the crowd.

I scanned the perimeter, and there he was -- looking right at me. "Shit." He was seated atop a "quad," one of those off-road vehicles that looks like a motorcycle with four wheels. I hoisted my pack up onto my shoulders and joined the line filing off the ferry.

"Welcome to Fantasy Island.' said McInnes and he handed me a coconut shell with a long straw and a flower sticking out the top.

"What's in it?"

"Nine kinds of rum and a little juice."

"I think five or six kinds would have been enough."

"Normally, perhaps, but this is a special occasion. The Adventure Brothers ride again!" We shook hands vigorously.

"Fellow Adventure Brother," I said in a somewhat solemn tone, "I bear bad news."

"Does it concern the untimely death of Ol' Creampuff?" I was momentarily taken aback. "How do you know about that?"

"Some of the tourists were talking about it. They spoke of a fair-haired American gardener who barely escaped with his life when his ancient station wagon, called "Old Muffin," rolled off a cliff. My guess was that it was you. Is it really true?"

"Yes. I'm sorry. I should have listened to you when you suggested we fix the brakes ..."

"Don't be silly; it was a noble death and she wouldn't have wanted to go any other way." For the next few minutes I sipped my rum concoction and described to McInnes, in vivid detail, the chain of events which led to the loss of our dear Ol' Creampuff. He listened intently and nodded constantly, silently expressing his approval and concurrence with my interpretation. When I had finished, there was a pause before he spoke.

"I'm going to ask you a favor," he said.

"Name it."

"In the future, when we tell the story of the dramatic passing of 01' Creampuff... may we say that I was there too?"

TEN

The Races, the Grand Piano, and the Cyclone

The "quad" upon which McInnes had been mounted when he picked me up at the ferry had been provided by his employer. So had his apartment, it turned out. It was high on a hill overlooking the marina, and, when we walked in, I had to laugh at Andrew's good fortune; which had just become my good fortune as well.

The apartment was white and airy and tropical, with straw mats on the floor, fans on the ceiling and doors that hadn't been closed for months. He pointed to an extremely comfortable-looking hammock on the balcony and told me that it was my bed.

"Perfect," I said. The sounds and smells of the marina below drifted up the hill and breezed through the apartment like whispers of invitation and it wasn't long before we succumbed and were heading back down so that McInnes could share with me the delightful decadence of Hamilton Island.

It was the first day of "Race Week." Boats from all over the South Pacific had come to participate in one of the southern hemisphere's most important nautical events. This explained the festive electricity in the air; although McInnes claimed that it was always that way anyway, just with fewer boats in the marina.

Hamilton Island, I quickly deduced, was a place where wealthy people went to get away from peers, employees and subordinates so that they could drop the act and release the wild idiot who'd been longing for months to get out. For this reason, I didn't feel unwelcome or out of my element anymore, as I had when the ferry first pulled into the marina. It was just a big party, I realized, and I could party with the best of 'em. The fact that many or most of them were millionaires merely meant that there were a lot of people on the island who could afford to buy us drinks.

McInnes had the week off as water skiing instructor because every available square meter of surface water surrounding the island was being used for sailboat racing. It was, therefore, playtime for us again. We walked along the docks on my first afternoon there, strolling from boat to boat with the intention of finding a skipper in need of two fine crewmen (although neither of us knew a damn thing about sailing).

We had a couple of offers right away from captains who were looking for only one person, but we had to decline, with polite regrets, of course, because the Adventure Brothers came as a package or not at all. When we were finally offered crew positions as a pair, it was by two boats simultaneously. We stood on the dock extending out between the two slips containing the big yachts, and we looked back and forth at the beckoning crews.

On our left was "Scorcher": 56 feet of hydrodynamics. She looked as sleek as a big surfboard; the only things disturbing her smooth profile being her mast and her gleaming winches. The tan, athletic-looking men on deck claimed that she had won her class the year before and had placed either first or second in every race she'd entered that year. Two of the regular crew members had not shown up and the honor of replacing them was available to us.

Our duty would be to crank the winches and adjust sail tension at the skipper's command. On our right was "Sea Slug": 58 feet long and about as smooth and sleek as the Manhattan skyline. She stood high above the water, cluttered with outcroppings, furniture, decorative windsocks, flags, and awnings. She looked more like an eccentric's townhome than a racing yacht and did not appear capable of hurrying.

The skipper and his crew all held beers and cocktails and they explained that they already had enough people on board to man the vessel, but that we were more than welcome to come along for the ride -- as long as we were in no great rush to get back. Our duty would be to help them drink as much booze as possible, and maybe pull on a rope now and then.

McInnes and I looked back over at the incredible "Scorcher" and her impressive crew, with their muscles and their water bottles, and then at each other. With a wave and a "thanks anyway" to those on the racer, we stepped aboard "Sea Slug." As it turned out, we did not race against "Scorcher." Even though we started the race at the same time, the two vessels were of different classes. "Scorcher" belonged to the unlimited class, while "Sea Slug" belonged to the cruiser class (which really should have been called the "party class"). The differences between the classes were amusing.

When the cannon sounded the start and the unlimited boats began to pull away, their crews could be heard barking orders at one another and crewmen were cranking winches like possessed human motors; while those in the cruiser class could be seen dancing on deck, raising glasses, and passing out sandwiches. I was sure that crewing on one of the serious unlimited boats had its good points, but, reclining there on "Sea Slug," drinking a cold beer and meandering through the turquoise waters of the Whitsunday Islands with McInnes and several other good people, I really couldn't think of one.

"Sea Slug" was aptly named. Five hours after starting the race, we crept across the finish without a single vessel behind us. We had given one other boat a run for its money; it was a similar cruiser which had torn its mainsail just a mile from the finish line and we'd nearly caught her. The crew had lowered the ruined sail, however, and raised a replacement just in time to maintain a slight lead and they all dropped their pants and waved their private parts at us when they edged us at the finish.

The races continued all week and we were invited to crew on "Sea Slug" every day. However, we always seemed to be racing against the same boats with the same results and I wondered once or twice what it was we were accomplishing. I eventually gathered that there were daily winners in each class who received small trophies at the end of each day, and then overall winners who would receive very tall trophies at the end of the week.

We were certainly in no danger of being awarded either, yet we were content with the fact that we didn't require a plastic figurine to confirm the amount of fun we were having (in fact, our sea motto, perhaps a bit over-used, was "Trophy? We don't need no stinking trophy!" delivered with a sour grimace and a cheap bandito accent).

When race week drew to a close, most of the boats inhabiting the marina, including "Sea Slug," sailed off in every direction and disappeared over the horizon and things went back to the way they usually were on Hamilton Island. McInnes had resumed his duties as water skiing instructor, which, I observed, consisted mainly of towing soft, rich people for short bursts until they either fell or it became obvious that they were never going to be able to get up on their skis (Andrew developed his back muscles by hauling large, bathing-capped women into the boat like a primitive whaler).

This usually kept him busy until four or five in the afternoon and gave me plenty of time of my own. I ran up and down the island's formidable hills for exercise, mingled with the guests at the resort and began working on a manuscript.

Writing encourages the thought process. Like a muscle, the mind must be exercised if it is to remain fit and agile. During my travels with McInnes, I had been doing very little reading or writing and had become intellectually out of shape. It was slow going at first, but as I developed a daily routine, spending four or five hours a day sitting with my pencil and pad at a picnic table on the beach, my mind began to thaw and the thoughts began to flow again.

Unfortunately, however, this new flood of thoughts and ideas brought with it memory montages and daydream streams and I did more reminiscing and self-analyzing than I did writing. One of the things I decided during the many thought storms was that I had not yet found what I had set out to discover on my trip; I didn't feel that I was any closer to being a man than I had been on the day I left the United States.

"Will I know when it happens? Or, if it's a slow process, will I be aware that it's taking place? Maybe it is happening, and I just don't see it. Perhaps if I were to fly home today and stroll into my mom's living room, she would look at me and say..."

"You know, Dave, there's something changed about you... something I can't really put my finger on. It's almost as though you're ... well... closer to being a man than you were when you left four and a half months ago."

"Who am I trying to kid?' I thought, "I still put sex in front of eating; I still spend most of my money on beer. Maybe I'm not as much of an asshole as I used to be, though. Maybe that's the first phase of development from boy to man. It's the asshole part that goes first. Yeah, that makes sense." I decided that day that I was going to concentrate very hard on not being an asshole.

At four o'clock on a breezy afternoon, McInnes jogged up to my beach spot and informed me that news of an approaching cyclone was sweeping the island and that many people were evacuating. Its name was "Aivu," and its winds out over the South Pacific were being clocked at a hundred and forty miles per hour.

"How long before it hits?" I asked, beaming with excitement.

"If it maintains its current speed and direction, it should strike at approximately six tomorrow morning."

"Does that mean that you'll have tomorrow off?"

"Yes. Not even the Adventure Brothers would be able to water ski in a cyclone." I thought about it for a moment, but dismissed the idea almost immediately because, as I mentioned earlier, I wasn't much of a water person.

"How should we prepare?" I asked, "I feel we should visit the piano bar and drink very dry martinis until the sun comes up." The piano bar was my favorite bar on Earth. At the center of all the smoke, rattan, ferns, palms and ceiling fans, was the grandest grand piano I had ever seen.

It was half an acre of gleaming black lacquer, producing tones as rich and smooth as the oldest brandy and just as intoxicating. Manipulating the keys was old Tom, a small, spent-looking man in thick glasses.

So dwarfed was he by the vast instrument that he looked like a midget steering a supertanker. Yet, never has there been a captain in such complete control of his vessel. The initial impression of incongruity at seeing such a slight person producing such mighty sounds was immediately dashed when he began to play.

From the triumph of a charging bull elephant, to the delicacy of a lone firefly's reflection on a pond at midnight, the little man wove a tapestry of emotion which entranced everyone in the room. He was amazing.

McInnes and I spent at least part of every evening sitting around the magic piano, sometimes staying well into the morning hours. Tom the master would continue to play as long as there was someone in the bar to listen. He liked McInnes and me and he would send us as many Bombay Martinis as we could hold.

He introduced us to the crowd every evening as "The Knights of Chivalry"; we would stand and bow, trying to look as chivalrous as possible and he would then play a song which he had dedicated to us; "Moon River," because of the line that goes "Two drifters, off to see the world...." We would sing this line along with him every night and then raise our martinis to him in salute. On that night before the cyclone, our man behind the grandest piano announced to the full room that the bar would remain open all night and that he would continue to play until either the storm had passed, or he and his piano had been carried off on a gust.

The rain began to fall at midnight and the wind started to show unusual power by two o'clock. At four, the lawn furniture beside the giant pool outside began to dance, so we moved outside as a group and threw every chair and table into the deep end to reduce the number of potential projectiles. At five-thirty, we were experiencing the wrath of Cyclone Aivu.

The crowd in the bar had dwindled to the three of us and the piano could no longer be heard over the roar of the wind and rain. Old Tom at the keys gave up and had one more martini with us before McInnes and I headed off to find a good spot where we could sit and watch the cyclone.

The sunrise did not produce the fiery colors I expected, but, instead, only a suggestion of gray below a sky of ominous, churning black. I had never experienced such a powerful wind (except in the presence of Lorie the Tasmanian, of course) and it was not possible to stand up straight without being pushed back violently.

We inched along — three steps forward, two back — hunched and squinting into the ferocious, roaring gusts and needling rain and finally arrived at our destination. The vantage point we had decided upon was a gazebo at the top of a small, grassy slope overlooking the marina. We chose this spot partly because of the view it offered and partly because, along with the gazebo structure itself, the table and benches beneath it were set in cement and would give us something solid to hold onto during the big gusts.

There was one point during the cyclone at which I was reminded of the scene in the Wizard of Oz when Dorothy is looking out of her bedroom window while her home (well, Uncle Henry and Aunty Em's home) is suspended in the center of the twister and all sorts of interesting things and people are zipping by, borne on the wind. Andrew and I didn't see any people blow by, but we did see an unhappy duck who was as close to breaking the sound barrier as he was ever going to come.

Several deck chairs and other bits of nautical paraphernalia, including a large rubber raft, came dangerously close to hitting us, but we kept our heads low and ducked beneath our respective benches when we had to. At seven in the morning the roof of the gazebo blew off in one piece and was sucked into the grey/black sky.

McInnes and I, still clutching our martini glasses because we had vowed to do so, looked at each other and laughed.

He leaned across the table between us to say something to me and I met him halfway in order to hear him.

"It's much nicer this way," he screamed, directly into my ear.

"What is?" I asked, hollering.

"The gazebo. It's much more livable without the roof, wouldn't you say?"

"Infinitely," I concurred, at the top of my lungs.

At nine Aivu was showing signs of weakening and the damage she had left in her wake was becoming visible. Several boats of various sizes had broken their reinforced moorings and were strewn on the beach like suicidal whales.

Trees were either broken, limbless, or gone and debris of all sorts littered the battered landscape. Many storefront windows facing the sea had been blown in and I could only guess as to the extent of the damage inside. Yet McInnes and I had emerged unscathed, and we still held our martini glasses proudly.

At 9:30 we clinked them together, victorious, and staggered up the hill to the apartment where we slept all day. Upon arrival back on the mainland, I immediately led McInnes to the rock under which I had stashed my money. Being careful to use the legs and not the back, I crouched and rolled the hundred-pounder off of my buried treasure.

Beneath the small boulder, right where I had left my money, was a letter. A note. I did not speak; instead, I involuntarily released a low, gurgling moan which sounded like the noise a child's pet toad would make when squeezed too hard by its young keeper. I lifted the multi-page note with unsteady hands.

"To whom it most certainly concerns: As you have by now deduced, I found your money. Allow me to begin by stating that your mistake was not in choosing this particular spot for your purpose -- it is, indeed, a fine hiding place, due, both, to the fact that the best ones are usually right under our noses, and also to the even simpler fact that this rock is really quite heavy and was exceedingly difficult to move.

You erred, my careless friend, when you chose to conceal your assets during daylight hours and in full view of a potentially nefarious fisherman -- being myself. I had been fishing from the dock for nearly two hours with three lines in the water and having absolutely no luck when I noticed you milling about over here under the trees. I keep a pair of relatively high-powered field glasses in my bag so that I may watch the boats leaving and entering the harbor while I fish, and, since your movements were becoming increasingly curious, I lifted the glasses and trained them on you.

When you came upon this weighty stone, it was quite clear that you had found what you were looking for and you immediately shed the burden of your rucksack and studied the monolith with great interest. You then produced a girthy roll of bank notes from your right sock, kissed it once and deposited it beneath the stone. It was less than five minutes later when you arrived on the dock, purchased a ticket for the eight o'clock ferry to Hamilton Island, and, again, relieved yourself of your cumbersome rucksack.

You sat down not three meters from where I stood and asked me if I had yet procured my dinner from the sea. I answered that I had not and you expressed your regrets. You then, quite unsolicitedly, shared with me an entertaining tale about the recent demise of a very special automobile (named after a pastry, I believe) and that you were on your way to tell your best friend and *Adventure Brother* of your mutual loss. The ferry then signaled its impending departure and you took your leave; not, however, before wishing me the best of luck and stating these words: '*Somewhere out there, sir, is a whopper with your name on it.*' Before your ferry had even left the harbor, the tip of my center rod nodded twice and then dipped violently. Thirty minutes later I reeled in the biggest kingfish I've seen in ten years and subsequently sold the impressive specimen to a local seafood restaurant for a small fortune. Having fished for most of my life, I must admit that I'm a superstitious sort and believe in the existence of "luck." I thank you for wishing me luck on that fine afternoon, and, although nobody will ever know if it actually helped or not, you were a gentleman for sharing a few kind words with a stranger.

You'll find your money at the same booth where you purchased you ferry ticket. I took the liberty of transferring it there because I felt that I may not have been the only one to witness your concealing it. The woman at the booth is an acquaintance of mine and will be expecting you. You may notice that five extra dollars have been added. Consider it a small token of my appreciation for your helping me catch my "whopper."

And now, my friend, it is my turn to wish you luck. Enjoy your travels and learn what you can. I hope you find whatever it is you're seeking.

A fisherman"

The nice lady in the booth was, indeed, expecting me, and she gave me a smile and a fat envelope containing the sum of eight hundred and five dollars. I thanked her profusely and asked her to pass on my thanks to the fisherman as well. As McInnes and I were walking away, she called after me,

"Maybe you should think about using a bank."

ELEVEN

The Old Soft Thumb

The absence of Ol' Creampuff was never more apparent than the morning when McInnes and I sat down with our belongings on the side of the highway and stuck out our thumbs. It was humbling for the Adventure Brothers -- former conquerors of the continent and spitters into death's eye -- to sit and facially plead for rides from passing motorists.

We had looked around Airlie Beach and neighboring Canonvale for a cheap used car, but with the prohibitive prices of new cars in Australia, small town folks held onto, and drove, any piece of shit which remained drivable. We felt that Townsville, a comparatively large sea-side city a couple of hundred miles to the north, represented a far better opportunity for us to find something suitable. Taking turns manning the thumb, we waited patiently for a decent Australian to take us to Townsville.

Hitch-hikers were not popular in Australia at the time due to a few bad apples who had murdered their drivers and spoiled it for the rest of us (also, a few hitch-hikers themselves had disappeared). The prospects, averaging about one every three minutes and being comprised of two trucks to every car, continued to ignore our nonverbal pleas. We

found it amusing how so many of the drivers found something within their car or truck to fiddle with in order to avoid
eye contact with us as they passed.

With absolutely nothing but time and topics, we chatted
about life and also developed our theories about hitch-hiking.
While I felt that a friendly smile should be employed to suggest to drivers a general lack of malice, McInnes had other
ideas...

"Although I've never actually been forced to do this, the
proper method strikes me as obvious. Our expression and
posture should indicate an air of nonchalance. We must give
the impression that we are certainly in no great need of a
ride, but if one were offered, we might consider accepting;
after, of course, inspecting the automobile and its occupants
for cleanliness and overall suitability.

The beckoning thumb should be presented very casually
and should lie almost flaccid; an erect thumb would indicate
over-zealousness and provoke mistrust. I can almost guar-
antee that, if we follow these simple guidelines which I've just
laid out, we'll be rocketing northward in a matter of
minutes..."

I humored McInnes and went along with his casual, limp-
thumb method of hitch-hiking, and we sat drooping in the
same spot for three hours. One of our continuing main topics
of discussion as we waited was "the people of Australia."
While McInnes held to his original view that it was a country
of uneducated, belching thugs, I had come to like the Australians. Their brashness and predictable method of charging
into a conversation offended Andrew, but I found it refresh-
ing. It was true that many could be described as "uncultured,"
but I admired and was attracted to their honest presentation
of themselves. No bullshit.

Growing up in L.A., I had come to expect to spend the first
few minutes of an introduction to a new face hacking through

the projected facade in order to locate the actual person in front of me. And sometimes I would never find them at all; they just turned out to be one big ball of shit from front to back and an utter waste of my time.

With an Australian, however, there was no question or doubt as to who the person in front of me was. The attitude, very basically, said "This is me. If you like me, let's have a beer. If you don't like me, then fuck you." There were some whom I did not like, but at least I knew who they were and I could say exactly why I didn't care for them. The girls were the same. If an Australian girl had any interest in getting to know me better, she would let me know. And, conversely, if she felt that I was an asshole, it would be clearly understood.

One thing I did find a little shocking about the Australian people was the way that the men viewed and treated the women. The pub was the working man's haven where the wife or girlfriend was not welcome. It was his home-away-from-her. He would meet his mates after work, spend whatever money he had brought and then stagger home expecting dinner to be ready.

And just as disturbing as the men's view of the women was the women's view of themselves. They have allowed the men to convince them into believing that they occupy a slightly lower rung on the evolutionary ladder. It was a Ralph Kramden mentality which didn't look like it would be changing any time soon.

A few minutes into our fourth hour of waiting for a ride, a man in a Toyota surprised us by pulling over. While McInnes dozed in the back seat, leaning on his leather luggage, I sat up front and attempted to build a conversation with the gentleman who had been kind enough to allow us into his car. It was futile, however.

Here was a man who had absolutely no interest in who Andrew and I were or what we were doing in Australia. This was certainly his prerogative, but I couldn't help but wonder why the hell he had picked us up. Most people, I felt, pick up hitch-hikers out of the goodness of their heart and also for a little human interaction to help pass the miles. The only question our driver ever asked me was "How far are you going?" When I told him that our destination was Townsville, he said, "Right." I understood that some people are shy and require some coaxing to get them out of their shell, so I pressed a little.

I volunteered information and shared what I thought were some pretty entertaining anecdotes, yet I was unable to arouse any interest or response. After nearly an hour of listening to myself talk, I was about to give up when the man to my right turned to me and said,

"Listen, friend, I realize that you're just trying to be polite by talking to me, but I'm really not in the mood for conversation. Why not just grab some shut-eye like your mate and I'll wake you up when we get to Townsville."

Well, needless to say, I felt like an asshole. I apologized for babbling and then did my best to take a nap. But I couldn't fall asleep. I felt that there was something wrong with dozing in a stranger's car when he had taken the trouble to pick us up and was doing us a great favor by driving us over two hundred miles. Even if he didn't want to talk, I felt that I owed it to him to stay awake.

I sat and stared out at the landscape and tried to relieve my discomfort by counting and appreciating the miles. It was almost three in the afternoon when we arrived in Townsville. Our driver said that he would take us to a used car lot (he knew that we were looking for a cheap car because that was one of the many pieces of information which I had disclosed to him during my 55-minute monologue).

However, before we had even penetrated the outskirts of the city, McInnes, who had just woken up, noticed a little white car on the side of the road with a "For Sale" sign in the window. It was parked next to a service station, so, after giving the car a quick look-over, we entered the garage to make our inquiries.

Twenty minutes and five hundred dollars later, we owned a 1971 Mazda Capella. It needed a couple of things, but its owner was also the owner of the garage, so we just wheeled it inside and incorporated the necessary repairs into the deal.

Strangely, the quiet, mysterious man who had given us the ride to Townsville waited in his car until we were all quite sure that we had a deal and that we would be able to drive our new Mazda away that afternoon. We couldn't figure him out. We asked him several times if he would allow us to buy him lunch or a beer, but he refused. He seemed to be deriving no pleasure from our company, yet he did not leave until we told him that we were okay and that we no longer required his help. And what he did then baffled us even more; when he pulled out of the petrol station, he got back on the highway heading south. We wondered how far he had gone out of his way for us. Whatever the man's reason was for helping us, whatever his motivation, McInnes attributed our good fortune to our flaccid thumbs.

It certainly possessed none of the charm or magic of Ol' Creampuff, but our new car was a car nonetheless and we were mobile again. It was a small, white, tired two-door; the sort of car which goes completely unnoticed unless driven by a beautiful girl with overflowing blonde hair.

It seemed to run well though and its little Japanese motor promised to consume far less gasoline than the burly main engine of its legendary predecessor. While Ol' Creampuff had been an automatic, making the switch from left-hand to right-hand drive relatively simple for me, our newly acquired Mazda boasted a stick shift and posed a new challenge for me: left-hand shifting.

I missed some shifts at first and did some serious gear grinding, but I caught on quickly and decided that if I just relaxed and pretended that it was easy, then it was easy.

Townsville was a clean, pleasant, sea-side city, yet a little dull because the rainy season had descended and the crowds were no longer migrating to the coast. There was still the steady flow of foreign travelers moving from city to city, hostel to hostel, and it was amazing how many familiar faces we came across; amazing because Australia is as big as the United States, and we ran into at least half-a-dozen people we'd met in other towns along the circuit.

Since the early days in Surfer's Paradise, the word among the travelers was that Cairns (pronounced "Cans") was the place to visit. It was supposed to be one big, beautiful party, and was many a traveler's ultimate destination. Cairns was just two hours north of Townsville by car, and, since we had just acquired one, we decided to blow Townsville and make Cairns before dark.

One hour out of Cairns, the little Japanese motor under the hood of our new Mazda coughed, sputtered, and died. McInnes traced the problem to a faulty fuel pump, and, after working on it for over an hour with a butter knife and a pair of tweaked needle-nosed pliers (the extent of our tool kit), he announced with a sigh that it would have to be replaced.

Without a fuel pump store in sight, we decided to sit on the hood of the car and have a beer and wait for something to happen. Less than two beers later, as the light was beginning to fade, an elderly gentleman in a big pick-up pulled up behind us and asked us if we were having problems with our car, or if we had just decided that this was a good place to pull over and drink some beer.

"Well both, really," I said. McInnes then explained to him what was wrong with our little Japanese fuel pump.

"That's a bitch," said the lean old man, who looked, spoke, and smelled like a farmer.

"You'll be needin' a tow then." At that, he climbed stiffly back into his tall truck, started it up with a roar, and positioned it in front of our little Mazda. He then produced a thick length of rope out of the back and proceeded to hook us up.

It was a good day for the Adventure Brothers in general, but it was an especially profitable one for Andrew McInnes. As I've mentioned, McInnes possessed an inbred habit of looking down his British nose at the Australians. On this particular day, two such "classless ruffians" had ventured great distances out of their respective ways to make our lives considerably better. The fact that they had performed these generous deeds caused McInnes to re-assess his outlook.

"Have I been a terrible snob?" he asked me.

"Yes. But I've enjoyed it."

"So have I; but from this moment on I'm going to give each and every man a chance to prove himself individually."

"And the women?"

"Depending upon how attractive they are, I'll give the women as many chances as I feel they deserve."

"That's very generous of you."

"Yes." With a new fuel pump a pumpin', we made it to Cairns late the next morning, after having slept in the car outside a garage where the Australian farmer had towed us. The little garage opened at eight, we had the new pump installed by nine and we pulled into Cairns at ten. As we drove through and around town, I felt as though all of those people who had raved so much about Cairns were part of a great conspiracy and had played a joke on us.

Cairns was made up of touristy gift shops, camera shops and souvenir stands, and, in my eyes, the city lacked any real civic personality. While Airlie Beach had been a charming residential settlement which had slowly developed into a quiet tourist attraction, Cairns looked more like it had been built for visitors.

Apparently, however, some of the world's best scuba diving could be done on the Great Barrier Reef just off the coast, but McInnes and I didn't care to invest the time or money necessary to become certified divers, so the town had little to offer us. It was a bit of a letdown, but we agreed to make the best of it and have some laughs anyway.

The hostel we found was actually one of the very nicest we'd seen. The owner was a man who respected his guests and expected the same in return, so it was clean, comfortable, and well run. McInnes and I had our own room, which was a welcome change from the "share accommodations" found at most hostels. We moved our belongings in, got organized, and set off to explore the area.

While the city of Cairns itself had not impressed us, the surrounding countryside certainly did. We drove north a little over an hour to a place called Mossman Gorge. It was spectacular; rugged, green, lush, healthy, and unspoiled. While McInnes napped on a towel at the river's edge, I went on the most enjoyable run I had ever been on. I charged along a narrow, winding trail through a jungle straight out of a Tarzan movie and felt like I should have been wearing a loin cloth instead of running shorts. I ran for an hour and then dove off of a giant boulder into the cool river. It was a perfect day.

After arriving back at the hostel and enjoying a good hour's nap, McInnes and I were in the common kitchen arguing about how to prepare spaghetti for our dinner. It was amazing how even the simplest task -- boiling noodles -- could provide fuel for heated discussion. A very attractive girl with short blonde hair was sitting alone at a table eating a salad and was obviously amused by our quibbling.

"You two argue like a married couple." Her accent indicated that she was from upper class England.

"Oh, we're not arguing," said McInnes. "My good friend David here has absolutely no idea how to prepare pasta and I was merely attempting to enlighten him."

"Excuse me for correcting you, Mr. McInnes," I retorted, "but you've selected the wrong verb. You were not attempting to enlighten me, you were trying to poison me. Perhaps in Scotland they like their spaghetti crunchy; however, in civilized countries we prefer it cooked until soft." Arguing with Andrew McInnes was always fun and the pretty English girl seemed to be enjoying it too.

Amanda was her name, and, once McInnes and I had settled our culinary differences by producing a colander full of spaghetti we could both accept, she invited us to join her.

She was petite and extremely feminine; her hair, clothes, posture, and attitude suggesting careful grooming and selective breeding. McInnes, who often mentioned the importance of a woman's possessing and projecting these very qualities, was clearly taken by her.

The spacious eating area next to the kitchen was set up restaurant-style, with ten or twelve rectangular tables spread evenly about the room. As it was getting late, the dining room was empty except for ourselves and a lone female diner seated three tables away from us. She looked a little bored.

"Would you mind if I asked that girl if she'd like to join us?" I asked Amanda.

"Certainly I wouldn't mind. The more the merrier." And then there were four.

Chris was from Alaska. Blonde, tan, and obviously fit, she shocked us when she told us that she was forty because she had the body of a twenty-year-old. Close inspection revealed a few wrinkles around the eyes and mouth, undoubtedly due, in part, to the extreme Alaskan weather, but she possessed an enthusiasm and a sparkle which contradicted her age as much as her hard body did. She was one of those women whom other women envy because of her seemingly everlasting youth.

It was obvious that a warm and friendly chemistry was developing among the four of us immediately and it wasn't long before we had made plans to go out together for the evening.

We chose to visit the town's most popular nightclub, but encountered a small problem when we tried to enter. I had worn a pair of jeans, oblivious to the fact that there would be a large man standing by the front door who was paid to prevent anyone clad in denim from entering. I didn't really feel like driving all the way back to the hostel just to change my pants, so we considered finding another club.

Back out on the street, next to a public bathroom, Chris voiced an idea.

"Why don't you wear my pants into the bar?" She was wearing the sort of pants that Barbara Eden used to wear as a genie; the kind of pants that no man should ever wear. They were silk, very baggy, and pink, with wide elastic bands at the waist and ankles.

"If I were to wear your pants, then what would you wear into the bar? If they wouldn't let me in in my jeans, then I'd say there's a pretty good chance they won't let you in in your panties, either."

She then outlined a fiendishly clever plan: She suggested that I go into the public men's room outside, remove my jeans in a stall, and give them to McInnes. Concurrently, she, Chris, would remove her genie pants in the ladies' room and give them to Amanda. Andrew and Amanda would then meet outside and exchange the pants.

McInnes would bring Chris's to me, and Amanda would bring mine to Chris. I would then don the silken lovelies, swish into the nightclub with McInnes, move promptly to the men's room, and remove them in a stall. Andrew would then take them back out to Amanda, who would bring them to

Chris, who would be waiting in or around the public ladies' room wearing my Levis. She would then switch in a stall again and the three of them would enter the nightclub with my jeans concealed in a purse or under a shirt. Andrew would sneak my jeans back to me in my stall and I would re-emerge in my own pants. Certainly, then, the club would be far too dark and crowded for anybody to notice that I wasn't quite up to dress code.

While I had to admit that the plan was an ingenious one, I had a slight problem with it. I wasn't wearing any underwear. This meant that I would not only have to "swing free" while wearing Chris's sheer silkies, but, after removing them, I would have to sit naked and wait in the nightclub's restroom for McInnes to return with my pants.

"What if something happens to you while I'm waiting and I end up stranded in there with nothing on but my shirt and my loafers?" I asked, genuinely concerned.

"What could possibly happen to us?" asked McInnes, "and, besides, we're the Adventure Brothers; you'll just be adding yet another manly accomplishment to a list of many."

I looked down at Chris's pink, puffy, bloomer-like pants and cringed.

"Manly?" I asked.

Ten minutes later I was walking up the steps to the night-club garbed in quite an eye-catching ensemble. From the waist up, I was relatively inoffensive, with a slightly wrinkled, light blue Polo shirt. However, all social acceptability stopped there. The pink genie pants looked utterly ridiculous on their own, but combined with my worn, brown loafers and my white, Irish ankles, I looked like an unemployed clown.

McInnes laughed every time he looked at me, so he averted his eyes as we approached the door so as to avoid attracting any more attention than I was already getting.

In my nervous, self-conscious state, my manhood had withdrawn somewhat and was not so much swinging freely as it was protruding unimpressively behind the thin veil of pink silk.

The elephantine goon who had stopped me earlier when I had been wearing man's pants eyed me disapprovingly. I tried to look as cool and as masculine as possible, and I did my best John Wayne walk as we passed him. Just as I was beginning to think that I had made it in, a heavy hand clamped on my shoulder. Caught, I looked up at the thuggish bouncer.

"Next time, mate," he said, "you're going to have to wear a belt with those." I was in.

Because Australia is a nation of beer drinkers, the country's leading engineers grouped together and designed a men's urinal which could accommodate large numbers of full-bladdered men at a time. The trough-style urinal does away with the slow-moving men's room line where grown gentlemen are forced to pinch their puds in agony like little boys because of poorly planned plumbing. However, the urinal which took up ninety percent of the bathroom wall left enough room for only one sit-down stall; and it was occupied. So I waited.

The bright florescent lights overhead really brought out the pinkness in my puffy pants, and, as the men filed in and out of the room, they glared at me and shook their heads. When the stall finally became vacant, I rushed in and closed the door behind me and felt a great relief.

"Mulligan, let's have 'em," said McInnes, sotto voce. He wasn't giving me any time to ease into what I was doing.

"Just a second, just a second." I stepped out of my loafers, took a deep breath, and removed Chris's pants. I then balled them up, and handed them under the partition to my snickering Adventure Brother.

Time has a certain elasticity to it, and, depending on how one is passing it, there are situations when minutes seem like hours. As I sat naked in the stall of that crowded men's room, time went limp and ceased to pass all together. The bottom of the partition surrounding me was unusually high above the floor, exposing not only my white Irish ankles, but also my white Irish calves. Compounding my great discomfort was the fact that the lock on the stall door was broken and, also, there was a two-inch gap next to the door where anybody who cared to could look in and behold my semi-nudity.

Roughly an eon later, as I was contemplating various painful methods of killing Andrew McInnes, I could see through the crack that there were several bodies milling around outside the stall.

"How much longer ya gonna be in there, Mate?"

"Not long; I'm nearly finished." I was beginning to perspire, and I thought I heard somebody say something about my bare legs. Another age elapsed.

Suddenly there were feet just in front of the stall.

"C'mon, what the hell are you doing in there?!" He banged his fist on the door, and it swung half-way open before I could stop it. Our eyes met briefly as I shoved the door closed again.

"The bastard's not wearin' any bloody pants!" The bathroom came alive with chatter.

"There's a fucking pervert in there!"

"How the hell did he get in here with no trousers on?"

"Let's thrash the bastard!"

I knew that it was only a matter of seconds before the mob would charge into the stall and beat the shit out of me. Panic stricken, I began to frantically pull toilet paper off the roll and wrap it around myself. I was going to have to make a run for it.

As I was making the final wraps of my toilet paper diaper and psyching myself up for my escape, I heard McInnes' voice among the mob.

"Pardon me, gents, I'm looking for a man who's not wearing any trousers."

"He's in there. What is he, a flamin' poofter?"

"No, quite the opposite. It seems he was servicing a young girl in a stall in the ladies' lavatory when they were discovered by an off-duty female bartender. When she rushed out to find a security man, our brave friend fled to the safety of the men's toilet. In his rush, however, he neglected to bring his trousers with him. His lady friend approached me in the hall and asked me if I had seen a fair haired, blue-eyed American who was naked from the waist down."

"McInnes!"

"Yes?"

"Give me my fucking pants!"

My jeans appeared under the door. I quickly put them on (after pulling off my paper improvisation) and stepped out of the stall, unsure of what my reception would be. The crowd parted for me, and I was patted on the back enthusiastically by close to a dozen men.

"Good on ya, mate!"

"Got one in the ladies' toilet, did ya?"

"Save a few Sheilas for us, will ya?"

I was a hero.

It turned out that I had been waiting in the stall with no pants for one hour and ten minutes. The policy at the club was that if one left the bar for any reason, he or she would have to wait in line again to re-enter. There were only ten or fifteen people in line when McInnes had left, so he saw no problem. However, while he had been making the switch with Chris, a wedding party of over a hundred had shown up, so

Andrew and the girls found themselves at the end of a slow-moving line which wrapped half-way around the block.

As the four of us stood at the bar waiting for our first drink, I felt that there was something I had to ask them.

"I need to know something, and I expect an honest answer. As you guys were waiting in line, knowing that I was going through Hell in there with no pants on, did you ever laugh?"

The three of them looked at one another and erupted into laughter. I knew all along that it was a stupid question.

TWELVE

The Foursome

Since Cairns wasn't the pot of gold at the end of the rainbow that many had said it would be, McInnes and I decided to head back down the road to Townsville and give it a whirl.

Our first choice had been to head further north along the coast to a place in the tropics called Cape Tribulation, but the rainy season had rendered the northern roads impassable to any vehicles not possessing four-wheel-drive ("Bullshit," we said, "01' Creampuff would have made it..."). When we asked Chris and Amanda if they'd like to accompany us to Townsville, we expected a polite rejection.

To our surprise and delight, however, they accepted enthusiastically. They had both been travelling alone and the camaraderie we had achieved during our two days together appealed as much to them as it did to us.

Our first instinct was to look for the local hostel upon arrival in Townsville, but the girls raised an interesting point. There is strength in numbers, they pointed out, and it was decided that the four of us might be able to rent our own apartment for about as much as we'd pay for a hostel. We wanted a place near the beach, so we began our search there.

The first place we stopped was extremely desirable, but the manager announced that he couldn't rent an apartment for any period less than one month. A month was too long, however; we were prepared to stay for only a week. On our way out the door, he stopped us. He couldn't stand to see money walk away.

"I've got one vacant apartment. I'll let you have it for ten nights at eighty dollars a night."

"The complex is virtually empty," McInnes said without blinking. "We'll pay you thirty dollars a night for seven nights. That's two hundred and ten dollars you wouldn't have seen otherwise."

"Out of the question," returned the manager. "Eight nights at sixty a night."

"Seven nights at forty, or we'll spend our money with one of your neighbors." McInnes was performing admirably.

"Well, I wouldn't want you to do that... Alright, seven nights at forty dollars, but you'll have to supply your own towels at that price."

"That's unsatisfactory. We'll need towels, too."

"I'll find it in my heart."

"And the morning paper as well."

"How about a crack in the jaw?"

"We'll settle for the towels."

While the apartment manager, in his dingy, beer-stained t-shirt, had been more than a little on the seedy side, the apartment he rented to us was anything but. Less than a year old, it gleamed like a display model which had never been occupied. The floors were clean, gray tile; the furniture and accents were a pleasant, diluted turquoise. Modern fixtures, big windows, tasteful wall hangings, transparent shower... The place was cool. We had left the realm of "hostel vermin" and had just become "tenants" with a very nice place. Sure, it was only ours for a week, but ours is ours and we would stretch every minute.

After the initial room-to-room, rush-through tour, there was an awkward pause when it came time to decide what the sleeping arrangements would be. There were two bedrooms. The room on the right contained two single beds; the one on the left, a sprawling king-size. As I was preparing to make a joke about McInnes taking the king-size bed and the girls and I taking one of the singles, the girls announced in unison "we get the big bed!" as they launched themselves onto it and staked their claim.

Throughout my entire life, and up to that very moment in Townsville, I had been involved in two platonic relationships with members of the opposite sex. One was with my sister, and the other was with my mother. By this I do not mean that I slept with every other girl I had ever known; I just tried to. Had my indiscriminate lust been reciprocated on every occasion, I would have been the possessor of a perfect record. But something was different among the four of us. As McInnes and I settled in our double-bedded room, the point was raised and discussed that, if we were to make sexual advances toward our pretty roommates, we may destroy the camaraderie which had congealed so naturally.

There was definitely a special bond between the girls and us; a magic which, we feared, might be lost if we were to acquire carnal knowledge of our fair counterparts. Yet the most compelling, or repelling, reason to abstain was the fact that they truly trusted us. The prospect of seeing great disappointment in their eyes kept us in our own beds. McInnes and I decided that the only way our relationship with the girls would escalate would be if they initiated the move.

Now, you must understand that this abstinence stuff was new territory for me. An individual may adhere to a concept of right and wrong, but this does not necessarily mean that this individual is not longing to do the wrong thing.

As I lay in my bed on that first night in our apartment, I held a quiet conversation with an old adversary.

"It seems like every time I check in to see how we're doin', you've become a little more like Richard Simmons. Do you know who Richard Simmons is?"

"Yes."

"Has he become your new guru? I remember when you used to like guys like Clint Eastwood."

"You just don't understand."

"Understand? What is there to understand? It's a simple matter of mathematics. I see two girls, two guys, and two bedrooms. Just ask 'em. You've got nothing to lose."

"That's not true. We have a nice friendship to lose. Those girls are our friends."

"Perfect. So the preliminary shit is already done. You won't even have to hassle with any foreplay..." The week in Townsville with the girls was ideal and never once did McInnes or I stray from the land of Platonia.

The spell was never broken and I, for one, was quite proud of myself. The days were spent lying on the beach (when it wasn't raining, it was warm and sunny), exploring the surrounding countryside, and even some of the islands offshore, yet we always returned to our comfortable nest in Townsville.

The nights were for dancing. The four of us often owned our own little square on the dance floor, yet, if Andrew or I met a girl in which we were interested, Chris and Amanda encouraged our pursuit. I must be totally honest, however, and admit that, had the tables been turned and the girls would have gone off with a couple of other guys, I wouldn't have been at all supportive. In fact, I would have been jealous and against the idea. They weren't the types to get too close to strangers, though, so this situation never arose. I was glad it didn't, because I never had to display my blatant double standard.

The sun passed across the sky for the seventh time over our Townsville apartment and the man in the dingy, beer-stained t-shirt gave us until five o'clock to be out. Pretty Amanda had obligations back down in Sydney, so, after a long, syrupy good-bye, she boarded a southbound jet and rendered us a threesome. Chris, however, had nothing special planned and chose to remain with us as we climbed back into our little Mazda to make the two-thousand mile, north-western trek to the city of Darwin.

Darwin is located on the northern tip of the continent (in the Northern Territory) and is where the great majority of the crocodiles congregate. They chose this area because of the many swamps one may find there. However, to reach the swamps of North-central Australia from North-Eastern Australia, one must cross a vast, intimidating desert where temperatures commonly exceed a hundred and thirty degrees. We were warned several times to bring plenty of extra water with us and we even heard a few stories about entire families who had perished in the heat after breaking down while crossing.

A sensible man disclosed the realities, however. He explained that, as few as ten years earlier, it had been quite dangerous to make the trek across the desert from Townsville to Darwin. But, back then, many stretches of the road had not yet been paved, and the rough, rocky surface was notorious for flattening tires or snapping important metal parts.

Also a decade earlier, there were not so many little shops along the road where one could stop to eat, drink, and refuel. There used to be, perhaps, four or five hundred miles of nothingness between settlements or fuel stops. Those days were gone and the entire length of highway had been paved, but the legends of sun-dried families lived on among travelers and added to the romance of the crossing.

On our way out of Townsville, when the terrain was still hilly, wet, and green, we stopped at a music store and bought ourselves a book containing the words to a thousand and one songs (actually, Chris paid for it because McInnes and I were running out of money again). Like Ol' Creampuff, the little Mazda did not possess a radio, and we thought it might add a nice dimension to our journey if we could sing our way across the desert.

THIRTEEN

Ant Posts and Scary Cows

It wasn't long before the roadside greens faded to browns, and the browns washed to rust; and then the earth went Martian-red. One day, many years in the future, a small group of astronauts will land on Mars. If one of them happens to be Australian (which is unlikely, because Australians are just not the astronaut types), I'm nearly certain he would draw a comparison, for all the world to hear, between the Martian landscape and that of the desert between Townsville and Darwin.

I can predict this because I've seen computer-enhanced images of the red planet and the only difference between what I saw in those and the terrain surrounding our Mazda was the presence of one billion ant hills. Spaced roughly twenty feet apart from one another and averaging about two and a half feet in height, the seemingly infinite number of ant hills dotted the red earth from highway to horizon and beyond. The ant hills that I had known in my youth were short and cone-shaped, like tiny volcanos.

These, however, looked like ancient, eroded fence posts. Perhaps they had been conical when the ants had first erected them, but the winds and rains had eventually worn them down to their cores. The ants and the elements had unknowingly collaborated in creating the eerie posts.

While the dangers of the old days — breaking down while crossing the desert and then shriveling in the sun - were no longer threats, there were new hazards even more ominous to the modern traveler. Though I never saw a single rancher, apparently much of the land through which we were threading was ranch land, and, in many areas, there were almost as many cattle as there were ant hills. Cows, in themselves, are not dangerous, unless they are bulls.

Any man who runs from a cow would probably also run from Richard Simmons. But they are quite large, and there were no fences separating their munching domain from the road. Therefore, they would drift across the narrow highway like hoofed icebergs, providing a deadly threat to any hapless Mazda and its occupants. On a flat, straight road, they would have been easy to avoid because they could be spotted well in advance. The road to Darwin, however, was dippy and meandering, so the utmost concentration and caution was required from whichever of us happened to be driving.

Quite often -- sometimes every couple of hundred yards— we would come upon a dead cow which had been hit. Most would be lying next to the road, although some would be in it, and all were in various stages of decomposition, ranging from freshly-nailed, to skeletal. And the smell... there's nothing like a hot, rotten cow to clean the ol' nasal passages.

Apparently, there was no "cow patrol" which would come along and scoop them up and this struck me as typically and refreshingly Australian ("Why the hell should we pick 'em up, mate? They'll be gone soon enough anyway when the vultures and the rats get a whiff of 'em").

Bloody kangaroos also dotted the road, and this I found very disturbing because I still had not seen one hopping. We pulled over a couple of times to get a close look at a dead one, but it just wasn't quite the same.

As threatening as the desert cows were, they were nothing compared to the infamous Road Trains. While the cows were passive objects waiting to be struck, the Australian road trains would barrel over yonder hill and right at us at ninety miles an hour.

Similar to the 18-wheelers of America's highways, the Australian road trains were taller, wider, and pulled as many as four trailers. It would have taken an awfully long time to stop or even slow a vehicle of that size moving at those kinds of speeds, so the drivers (or "engineers") never bothered to touch the brakes.

The road belonged to the road trains and anything in the way would be destroyed (which explained the great numbers of dented cattle along the shoulders). Even a massive road train would sustain damage from smashing into a 1,200-pound cow at speed, so they were all equipped with extra heavy-duty metal framing bolted to their noses to deflect the unfortunate bovines. They were called "bull bars" and were often bent and contorted from serving their purpose.

In between dodging clueless cows and swerving off of the narrow road to avoid the raging road trains, we made steady progress across the desert. While we had started out enthusiastic about using our song book with its one thousand and one songs, it turned out that about nine hundred and ninety-eight of them were ones that McInnes nor I had ever even heard of. Chris, being several years our senior, was familiar with many of them, but she couldn't carry a tune to save her life so it was impossible for her to convey them to us.

None of us could read music, either, so out of one thousand and one songs, were able to salvage "Singin' in the

Rain," "Yankee Doodle Dandy," and "On the Good Ship Lollipop." I'll go to my grave knowing every word to those three songs.

FOURTEEN

The Northern Territory

The further north we drove, the wetter the air and the greener the earth became. Still several miles south of Darwin, we came upon a very large sign which read "Kakado National Park." Chris produced her traveler's guide (an item which McInnes nor I never would have had the sense to purchase) and read aloud about Kakado.

The words described a fascinating nature reserve covering hundreds of square miles, made up of land and swamp, and inhabited not only by crocodiles, but also water buffalo and countless other wild species.

It sounded like the sort of place that Marlin Perkins used to send his sacrificial sidekick Jim into to wrestle big game, the sort of place every closet adventurer dreams of visiting. But, after having just made the marathon, three-day desert crossing and singing the same three corny songs over and over until we began to feel sick, we needed to find ourselves a room with beds in it where we could fully recline and get some distance between one another.

Our plan was to get settled and relaxed in Darwin and we'd explore Kakado later when the time was right. Darwin's humid, salty, sleepy atmosphere reminded me of a mid-sized, South Floridian coastal town in the off-season (except there weren't lots of old, Jewish people driving in the wrong lanes and using their left turn-signal just before turning right).

Chris's guidebook claimed that Darwin is one of Australia's busiest ports of entry, but the town itself gave no indication of notable activity of any sort. Yet we welcomed the unhurried pace. If the town would have been bustling, we would have been somewhat overwhelmed in our road-weary state. Our introduction to Darwin was smooth and seamless because our collective pulse matched that of the city.

We chose a motel because it was dirt-cheap and because they had a room with three beds in it. It was no later than eight p.m. when our heads hit pillow and the three of us slept until almost noon the following day. Chris, then, set off to visit a crocodile farm, while McInnes and I devoted the afternoon to finding work.

While I had, in a sadistic, boot-camp sort of way, enjoyed my position as a gardener in Airlie Beach and felt that I had greatly improved my personal work ethic, I did not want another job where I would go home at the end of each day with dirt in my ears.

But, more than that, I wanted a job where I could talk to people. I wanted to meet more Australians. I was beginning to develop an overall impression of them, as a brash, honest, laughing, drinking, tough, and volatile people, yet I wanted to delve deeper. I wanted to work in a place where I could mingle with them. I wanted to work in a bar.

McInnes, on the other hand, felt that he knew all he needed to know about the Australians. He had no desire to attempt to merge with the local culture, because, in his eyes, there wasn't one. So he kept his distance. Andrew traveled at a "higher altitude," soaring above Australia as an observer.

However, he was a male with basic male needs, and he said to me as we embarked on our job hunt:

"Mulligan ... I realize that I said I was going to try not to be such a snob. I've attempted to communicate with the natives on a verbal, superficial level, yet I've been unable to muster any sort of literate response. Any good ambassador must be flexible in his struggle to mix with the locals. The most beautiful thing about the simple act of sex is that it knows no cultural boundaries. I'm going to have to try and communicate with them on a physical level. Perhaps working in a pub will be the best place to start."

There were countless bars in Darwin, yet the seasonal lull in business left many of the bar managers in positions where they were forced to lay off employees. And there we were, looking for jobs. We were told several times that we didn't stand a chance of finding any work, yet we were broke so we didn't have any choice. We pressed on against the current.

It was at least our tenth stop when we came to the Atrium Hotel. On the outside, it was white, new, and angular, and rose about ten storeys. But, quite unexpectedly, walking through the front door was like walking into a giant terrarium.

First of all, it was wide open, all the way to the skylights over a hundred feet above. Clinging plants and vines hung from the ascending interior balconies and giant potted plants and trees flourished all throughout the lobby. Adjacent to the front desk and reception area was an open restaurant and bar and this is where McInnes and I headed immediately.

We'd learned that dealing with personnel departments was just an invitation to bureaucracy, so we went directly into the bar and asked to see the manager. The man in charge was fortyish and friendly. When we announced that we were there looking for work, he invited us to sit down with him and have a beer (McInnes and I exchanged hopeful glances because we took this as a good sign).

It was clear that he just wanted to see what kind of guys we were, and he asked us general questions to get an idea of what our overall attitudes toward other people were. He also asked us about our bar and restaurant experience and what we would do in certain hypothetical situations, such as "what would you do if you were working behind the bar and a customer began to look as though he'd had a bit too much to drink?" He directed that one to McInnes, who, although he'd no bar experience, answered as though he'd been a bartender for years.

"As diplomatically as I was capable, I would apologize to the gentleman for having over-served him, and then suggest that he try something non-alcoholic, such as coffee or a soft beverage. Discretion would be vital so as to avoid embarrassing him. If he became angry or hostile and threatened to bother the other guests, however, then I would summon security and have him removed." The manager then asked me,

"What would you do if you were serving a beautiful woman who was staying here at the Atrium and she invited you to come up to her room after you'd finished your shift?" I paused. I didn't know whether I should lie or tell the truth. There are certain situations, I felt, that call for dishonest responses. Like when your girlfriend asks, "Have you ever had lustful thoughts for another girl since we met?" Even though you both know that you have, any man with an interest in keeping his relationship will answer "Of course not, dear." I then looked the manager right in the eye and said,

"I would decline in the politest way possible." He looked at me and smiled.

"Is that really what you'd do, mate?"

"No." He chuckled. "I appreciate your honesty. Situations like that are bound to come up. A man's got to do what a man's got to do. I was a bachelor myself not so long ago. If it happens, just keep it to yourself. If I find about it, I'll have to give you the sack."

"Does that mean that we're hired?" I asked.

"I had three employees leave yesterday without giving me notice. You've got the job if you can both show me a work permit." I had anticipated this. I'd learned to respond when I found myself in this situation by saying that my father was Australian and, therefore, it was legal for me to work in the country because I had dual citizenship. Unfortunately, I would continue, all of the paperwork was in Perth, where my father supposedly lived and he was visiting America at the moment. I would supply the necessary documents when he returned in two weeks. Hopefully, by the end of that two week period, I would have established a rapport with the management and we could work around the nationality problem.

"Well, I suppose that'll have to do." he said, and McInnes and I were employed. He gave us menus to study and we were to start the following day on the lunch shift. The two of us would alternate with one another daily from waiter to bartender. Before we left, he had us fill out job applications as a technicality.

Back in the hotel room, not thirty minutes had passed when there was a knock at the door. Chris was still out. McInnes, I pointed out, was closer to the door than I, so he answered it. I couldn't see who it was but I heard the conversation.

"G'day. Are you David Mulligan?"

"I'll tell you whether or not I am after you've told me who you are."

"I'm Jim Peete and this is Ian Sweeny. We're from The Department of Immigration."

"In that case, no, I'm definitely not David Mulligan," said McInnes. I was sitting up on my bed, around the corner from the door and out of our visitors' line of sight. I remained outwardly silent, yet inwardly I let out a loud "Oh fuck."

"You must be Andrew McInnes then," continued officer Jim Peete.

"Yes I am. How can I help you gentlemen?"

"Well, first we'd like to see some identification, then we'd like to speak with Mr. Mulligan."

"I'll show you mine if you show me yours," answered McInnes. I then heard the unmistakable sounds of two men showing their identification.

"Thank you," said McInnes. "Your credentials seem to be in order. Now, here's mine, as promised. Unfortunately, however, Mulligan isn't in. He's currently on an expedition in Kakado. Is there a message you'd like to leave for him?"

"When do you expect him back from his 'expedition'?"

"I've no idea. Sometimes he's gone for weeks at a time."

"But he's expected at work tomorrow."

"He's very irresponsible," said McInnes.

"Do you mind if we come in and have a look?"

"Yes, I'm afraid I do mind. The place is an absolute mess, and I'd find it very embarrassing."

"Alright," said officer Peete. When Mr. Mulligan comes back from his 'expedition', please have him call me at this number (I then heard the unmistakable sound of one man handing his business card to another). If we don't see him at the Atrium Hotel tomorrow, we'll come back. And tell him not to try and leave the country without talking to us, because he'll be arrested if he tries to get through immigration."

"I'll be sure he gets the message." McInnes closed the door and came into the room. "Looks as though we may have a slight problem," he said.

"It's not our problem, it's my problem," I answered.

"Nonsense. We stand together as The Adventure Brothers and as the Knights of Chivalry." I was certainly concerned, but I wasn't scared. I knew that the worst thing that could happen to me would be to get deported. My strongest emotion was frustration. There was still so much of Australia we had to see. Our plan had been to drive all the way around.

Obviously, the immigration officers had somehow found out about my applying for a job, and I was in for some trouble. It would be silly for me to make a run for it because they had my full name from my application and a red flag would pop up as soon as an immigration official entered my name on the computer at the airport. I talked it over with McInnes for a little while, and then decided to call the number on the card and meet the problem.

The first thing the agents asked me when they arrived back at our motel room was about my Australian father who lived in Perth. I knew they had access to any name they wanted, so I decided not to waste anybody's time by lying. I told them that it had all been a story, and officer Peete said,

"Well, it looks as though you have a problem then." Twenty minutes later I was in downtown Darwin, seated across a desk from Officer Peete's superior, who happened to be a woman. She appeared to me to be half-black, half-white, with creamy skin the color of milk-lightened coffee, and she had the most hypnotic emerald green eyes I had ever seen. I was honest with her, as I had been with her subordinates, and she appreciated this.

She looked a healthy thirty-five, was clearly an intellectual and was even more attractive when she spoke than she was when reading my file to herself. Her name was Dawn. I liked her. She knew I liked her.

"I hope you don't mind my asking," I said, "but what do you have in your blood that's given you that lovely skin and those eyes?"

"I don't mind at all. My mother is an Aboriginal."

"And your father?" I asked.

"Isn't," she said, smiling. Andrew and I had been exposed to many Aboriginals since entering the Northern Territory and we quickly learned that they are a race with serious problems. Not unlike what has been done to the Native American in the States, the "Abo's," as the locals called them, have been forced to watch their culture be engulfed by that of the Whites and they have become an endangered race. Australia has turned its back on them and appears to be doing its best to pretend they do not exist. The unemployment level among them is astronomical, and many have withdrawn into themselves and settled for a sedate life in an alcoholic fog. They are commonly seen singly or in groups lying on the side of the road or sleeping in the shade beneath trees. It's another sad case of white progress devouring everything in its path.

Just as I had been with her, Dawn was honest with me about my situation. I had broken the law. Even though I had not actually been caught working, they had my job application as tangible proof that I had sought employment and that was enough to have me deported. I told Dawn that, while it was certainly unfortunate that I had to leave, I was looking forward to seeing New Zealand, which was the next stop on my adventure. Her look told me that there were complications.

"Unfortunately, David, when one is deported from one country, no other country will allow them entry across their border. You'd be passed along and the only country which could accept you would be your own."

"Are you saying that I have to go home?"

"I'm afraid so."

"When?"

"As soon as it can be arranged." I was in shock. "Isn't there any way around this?, I mean, can't I go to jail for a while or something? I'll pick up trash on the beach. I'll do anything." She chuckled at me. "I really am sorry. There's no way to reverse what you've done."

"Can't you just allow me to leave? What if I just get on a plane tomorrow and go?"

"It's not that simple."

"Why not? You're the boss here, aren't you? Just let me go and I give you my word I'll be on the next plane out of here."

"I'm not actually the boss. The delegate above me is, and he already knows about your case."

"Well, may I speak with him?"

"No. He'd never agree to see you."

"You're sure?"

"Positive," she said, with finality.

"Would he read a letter from me?"

"He might, if he's not too busy. I'd be lying if I told you I thought it would do any good, though."

"That's alright, I've got to try. I can't go home yet." I was released while my case was being processed and there was no worry of my escaping because the lovely Dawn had confiscated my passport.

Actually, even if she hadn't taken it from me, I wouldn't have left because I gave her my word that I wouldn't and I could never lie to a woman with eyes like that. She informed me that it may be as long as two days before my papers were processed and suggested that I stop by the office each afternoon so that I would be ready when it was time for me to leave.

I secretly wished that the reason she wanted me to stop by each day was because she enjoyed my company, but I could see in those shimmering emerald eyes that she had no romantic interest in me. Even so, I fantasized about spending my remaining moments in Darwin with her as my partner.

When I arrived back at the motel, I found Andrew wearing a look of proud British defiance and Chris one of genuine concern. Chris was packed and ready to leave Darwin and had just waited for me to return so she could hear my fate and say good-bye to me. She was sorry that I was going to have to cut my trip short and head back to the States, but, at the same time, relieved that I wasn't in any real trouble other than that. We drove her to the airport, shared a few beers together as we re-lived some of our adventures, then watched her board a jet bound for Perth.

In our motel room once again, Andrew and I decided that the only chance I had to avoid being deported was to put pen to paper and write to Dawn's superior. I was going to plead my case and Andrew McInnes was going to be my character witness.

While my letter was a rather flat, straight, admission of guilt and a plea for leniency, McInnes produced a letter which described a man whom I'd like to meet someday.

"To whom it may concern: Mr. David Mulligan is, without a doubt, the finest man I know. Possessing the heart of a Saint, the wit of a poet and the intellect of a classic Greek philosopher, here is a man you should be proud to have gracing your soil with his presence. His generosity is unmatched. He is a fountain of good will and of benevolence. And now he is perched on the brink of catastrophe. The adventure upon which he embarked some five months ago is dangerously close to being transformed, by your hand, into misadventure. Technically, yes, he did break the law. However, in the two hundred years since the birth of this great nation, the men of this land have reached a level of civilization equal to any society on the globe; and a truly civilized man does not judge by the letter of the law, but by its spirit and the intention its authors had at the time of its inception.

Certainly, you could not allow every visitor from every country to have free and easy access to the finite number of jobs available in your great country; they are, indeed, national treasures which you have every right and obligation to protect for your citizens. Yet, David Mulligan did not come here with the intention of stealing anybody's job. There was no "Position Vacant" sign in the window where he sought employment. He approached the man in charge and created the vacancy by the strength of his character and the presentation of his self. He is a citizen of the world with much to offer. Please find it in your heart to show him leniency. The law is not carved in stone, but, instead, inscribed in clay. David Mulligan is deserving of a little subjective interpretation. I thank you sir. I am...

Andrew Cameron McInnes, Scotland." Andrew and I hand-delivered the letters to Dawn on the following afternoon and she suggested that she read them before her boss did because she may be able to make some suggestions as to their content. She read mine first and said it was just fine.

She read Andrew's letter wearing an amused grin and, when she'd finished, she said that I was lucky to have such a good friend. Of course, we then told her that we were much more than mere friends and gave her the unabridged version of the Adventure Brothers and Knights of Chivalry. She laughed and laughed and looked more beautiful than ever.

"It sounds as though you two have had quite an adventure," she said.

"We were just getting started," I said. Dawn then stood up from her desk chair and closed the door to her small glass-walled office. She began speaking before she was seated again.

"In my four years with this office, I've never let anybody go, or applied "subjective interpretation," as Mr. McInnes might put it. When I told you, David, that I'm not the boss here, I was telling the truth; however, I've earned my superior's trust over those four years and he now respects any executive decision I make without questioning it. In fact, he's grown old and tired and I don't think he even reads my reports anymore. After meeting with the two of you and seeing what kind of person you are, David, I'm going to agree with

Andrew's opinion that the law is not carved in stone. You don't strike me as the typical "illegal," and I think that you've given Australia as much as you planned to take. You say that you're working on a manuscript about your adventure, and I'd really hate to see your story end in Darwin." I couldn't believe what I was hearing. "You mean you're just going to let me go?"

"Oh no, I couldn't do that. I'm going to allow you four days to leave the country voluntarily."

"Does that mean that I'll still be able to go to New Zealand and the islands?"

"Yes. You're not being deported. You're being told to leave voluntarily."

"But why four days?" I asked.

"I've seen your plane ticket. Your flight will leave from Melbourne and it's going to take you close to three days on a bus to get from here to Melbourne. I know that you two own a car, but I'm going to suggest that you sell it here in Darwin and take a bus to Melbourne instead of driving. That way I know you'll get there on time. You'll still have half-a-day to allow for any possible complications. You can call and make your flight reservations today."

"When does my four-day clock start ticking?"

"It already has," she said.

"What are you doing tonight?" I asked.

Here's Your Passport, What's Your Hurry?

The next morning at eight, Andrew McInnes and I were standing out on the busiest road in Darwin trying to sell our car. We had procured a large sheet of plywood, white-washed it, and then, on it, boldly painted the words: "DEPORTATION LIQUIDATION." Beneath this we added the pertinent information in smaller letters:

"Good Runner"

"Current Rego" (the common term for registration)

"A steal at $600"

"A Real Creampuff" (this was stretching the truth a little; of course, there was only one real Creampuff). There were, perhaps, half a dozen other parties with cars for sale within the same block. All were travelers like ourselves. Most of them had reached the end of their Australian tour and were there to sell their car before boarding a plane to their next destination.

Most had small, hand-written cardboard signs on their windshields and they looked rather pitiful next to our five by-six-foot billboard. We mingled with the other selling parties and it was clear that they all envied us for our fine sign.

By noon we had sold the little Mazda for the full $600, and we had the money to pay for our bus tickets (which turned out to be $200 apiece, leaving me with just over a hundred dollars in my pocket). At two o'clock we boarded a big Australian cruiser bus (with a bathroom on board, I made sure) and we were on our way to Melbourne.

At approximately 11:00 p.m. I was the only person on the bus, other than the driver, of course, who was awake. I was working on the chronicle of my adventure by the dim glow of the light over my seat, when something rather scary took place. The driver hit the brakes very suddenly and then there was a loud crash followed closely by a heavy thump and a shock wave which reverberated through the bus.

My head bounced harmlessly off the seat in front of me and, a moment later, I was on my feet attempting to see what had happened. Others, including McInnes, stirred in their seats and looked around, bleary-eyed, as they awoke and I made my way to the front of the bus to find out what we had hit.

The driver was calm, as though nothing out of the ordinary had taken place, and I asked him what had happened.

"We hit a fucking bull. A big bastard, too. He rolled up on the bull bars and broke my windscreen." The center of the windshield was spider-webbed and slightly concave, with several of the cracks extending all the way to the frame. There were also dark spots and streaks on the glass which I took for blood. The irritated driver gradually brought the bus to a stop on the shoulder and got out to check the extent of the damage.

McInnes and I also got out and walked back to the have a look at the bull and confirm its deadness; it had, indeed, mooed its last moo. I felt sorry for the big animal, but I made a couple of quick hamburger jokes anyway and got back on the bus.

For the next six hours, we crept southward across the desert at thirty-five miles an hour. Traveling any faster would have been to risk blowing the windshield in. The driver radioed ahead to the bus station in the next town so that they'd be ready with a replacement windshield. Unfortunately, the heater pipes had been severed in the collision and there was no longer any heat on the bus.

Desert nights can be as cold as mountain nights and we, the passengers, shivered in our seats and donned our warmest clothing in an attempt to stay warm. Cold drafts swirled around our legs and down our necks. It was a long night.

In the next town's little bus station, all they were able to do was remove the smashed windshield and replace it with a temporary sheet of plexiglass. They lacked the parts and the personnel necessary to repair the heating system, and we were informed by our driver that we would be making the rest of the trip without one.

At ten o'clock in the morning on May the 1st, we pulled into Melbourne, completely exhausted. McInnes and I went directly to the regional manager of the bus lines at the Melbourne station and demanded our money back. We had spent three and a half miserable, sleepless days on that piece-of-shit bus without so much as a blanket or a "sorry for the inconvenience" offered to us. The temporary windshield they'd installed didn't fit and we'd spent the entire trip, from the top of the continent to the bottom, sitting in a wind tunnel.

Incredibly, the district manager of the bus company refused to refund our money -- until, that is, I threatened him with writing a letter to a friend of mine who worked for the Travel Section for the Los Angeles Times and that I would make sure and enlighten everybody in the city of Los Angeles to the fact that this man was an asshole and his bus company was run by an army of assholes and his buses were rolling turds driven by assholes and that if any one of the ten million people in the greater Los Angeles area was planning to visit Australia during his or her lifetime, he or she should consider using one of the competing bus lines. Probably just to shut me up, he gave us each fifty bucks and told us to "fuck right off."

Other than the partial refund, two noteworthy things came about as a result of my being on the Bus From Hell for those three days. One was, I wrote over twenty pages in my manuscript. I found it amazing how clear my mind could be at the strangest times; like 3:30 in the morning under a feeble light, in the middle of the Australian outback, facing a frigid twenty mile-an-hour headwind... and my hand couldn't write fast enough to keep up with my mind. I felt wonderfully productive.

And the other noteworthy event which took place was, I saw my kangaroo. It, too, was in the middle of the night, and, once again, I was the only conscious passenger on the bus. I had quit writing for the night and I did not yet feel sleepy, so I walked up to the front of the bus to talk to the driver, whom I liked. I sat in the front row, just behind and to the left of him, and we talked quietly about each other's country.

The first two rows of seats were empty because of the cold wind whistling by the ill-fitting plexiglass windshield, but I had on three shirts, two pairs of sweat pants and a towel wrapped around my head like a turban. During a short lull in our conversation, I stared at the road ahead, slightly hypnotized by the broken, unrelenting white line coming at us. Some color and movement ahead and to the left of the road brought me back and, when I focused, I realized that I was looking at a big kangaroo in full hop. He was alone, hopping parallel with the highway and I could see him quite clearly, as he was well within the field of the bus's high beams.

"Wow! That's a kangaroo!" My turban was pressed against the window as we roared past him and my eyes and mouth were open wide. And then he was gone. It had happened so quickly, my first impulse was to question whether it had happened at all. "That was a kangaroo I just saw, wasn't it?" I asked the driver.

"Sure was, mate." I suppose "anticlimax" best describes my feeling as I stepped from the realm of "those who've never seen a kangaroo" into that of "those who have." It was not a step up, as I had subconsciously figured it would be; it was merely another step forward, marking the passage of time. I was no different. No better. Just older.

I didn't just feel older, I was older. The day we arrived in Melbourne, the First of May, 1989, happened to be my twenty-seventh birthday. I've always been the type who tells everybody it's my birthday when it's my birthday. I was never the sort who would drop hints a week or two before my birthday in the hopes of being honored with a surprise party or lots of gifts. I just liked telling everybody on the actual day so that I would receive special recognition and feel like it was my day.

At that point, however, McInnes was the only person I had told. I was just too tired to tell everybody on the bus and in the station. After we had received our partial refunds from the bus company, McInnes and I reclined on a long bench in a quiet corner of the station. It felt wonderful to be able to stretch out after three days on the bus, and it wasn't long before both of us were dozing.

An hour or so later, I opened my eyes and discovered an elderly, well-dressed woman standing above me, eying me sympathetically.

"You poor boy. You look awfully tired."

"I am. And it's my birthday."

I then sat up and noticed that McInnes had left his end of the bench. This didn't surprise me; he always required shorter naps than I. In his place was a brief note, penciled on the side of a flattened paper cup. "I'm showering. Sleep on, Adventure Brother."

The elderly woman, still standing above me, spoke again.

"Are you a Canadian?" People asked me this frequently because a Canadian accent is so similar to an American, and Canadian tourists far outnumbered "Yanks."

"No. I'm an American."

"And how old are you today, dear?"

"I'm twenty-seven," I said, pitifully, seeking some more of her sympathy.

"Oh, you poor darling. You're the same age as my son, and you look so much like him. What's your name?"

"Dave."

"Here, look at his photograph and see how much you look alike." She sat down on the end of the bench where McInnes had been and opened her big purse and dug inside. ("Payday"), I thought to myself, ("I look just like her son"). I was well aware that no elderly woman can resist a young man who looks just like her son (unless, of course, her son is an asshole).

I heard jingling and she produced a heavy key chain with too many keys hanging alongside metal rings, a bottle opener, and three or four photographs immortalized between sheets of clear plastic.

"Here he is," she said, smiling lovingly at the image of her son, "that's Hilton with his wife at their home in Sydney. That's where I'm going." I leaned closer to her and looked at the picture of her son. He actually did share some of my features, but it was Hilton's wife who caught my eye. She was gorgeous. She was in a pair of cut-off jeans and a bikini top. She looked like Farrah Fawcett at twenty. When I realized that what I was doing was despicable, I handed her keys back to her.

"We do look a bit alike," I said. "He's better looking than I am though. Are he and his wife still together?" (I suppose that I asked this with the faintest of hopes that she would respond by saying "no, they divorced some time ago. I do have her address, though, if you'd like to meet her.")

"Sure they are. Say, are you hungry David? Have you had your lunch?"

"Well, not yet, but..."

"Say no more, I've got some sandwiches here I was bringing for Hilton, but I just do that for laughs anymore. He's got heaps of money." She reached into another of her many bags and brought out a bulging lunch sack.

"I don't want to eat Hilton's lunch..." This was a lie. I was starving. I wanted Hilton's lunch more than I wanted Hilton's wife.

"Hush now. I think he just throws them out anyhow. You eat these."

"Well ..."

"And you'll need a beer to wash them down." She was elbow-deep in her bag again, and surfaced with a big can of Fosters. My heart leapt. This woman was straight out of a fairy tale. I was so hungry and tired and I was trying to save the few dollars I had left. Then suddenly, sandwiches and beer. It was a meal I'll never forget. There were four sandwiches in all; I stopped when I'd finished two of them because I felt I should save the other two for McInnes. I wasn't so generous with the beer, however. I drank all of that. When McInnes re-appeared, looking refreshed, I introduced him to my Fairy Godmother and gave him the two remaining sandwiches.

She then produced another Foster's from her bag for Andrew, and I watched him enjoy Hilton's lunch as much as I had.

McInnes and I had been avoiding the subject, but it was inevitable and the time had come to address it. Our time together was coming to an end -- at least temporarily. We'd always planned on visiting New Zealand together, but, with my earlier-than-planned departure, circumstances had obviously taken an unexpected turn.

I had to leave Australia and Andrew couldn't leave yet. He had left some of his clothes and belongings with some friends of his family in Sydney with whom he'd stayed upon arriving in Australia and he had to go there before he could leave. He'd also promised them that he'd stay with them for a few days before leaving the country.

My flight into New Zealand would bring me to Christchurch, the largest city on the South Island. It was supposed to be pretty and quaint, like an old British city. And we'd heard many travelers speak of Queenstown, a mountain city, also on the South Island and every time we'd heard it mentioned we also heard about the bungee jumping there.

Bungee Jumping was the latest craze and McInnes and I decided that we'd meet in Queenstown exactly ten days after the day of our separation and celebrate our reunion by doing a tandem bungee jump off of the three hundred-foot bridge we'd heard so much about. That was our plan.

My flight from Melbourne to Christchurch was scheduled to depart at 4:00 pm. The airport was just a quick shuttle ride from the bus station, so I still had a couple of hours to relax with Andrew before I had to go. He had decided to take a bus to Sydney that same afternoon, so he'd be staying at the bus station until his bus left at five. We found a nice bar just around the corner from the station and sat down to have our last Australian beers together.

Saying good-bye to Andrew McInnes was bitter/sweet. While we certainly complimented one another, and had become the very best of friends, I had not originally set off on the trip with the intention of spending the entire time with a partner. It would be good for me, I felt, to be on my own for the ten days that Andrew and I would be apart. I liked the fact that I would be forced to become settled in New Zealand on my own, as opposed to relying on the strength of The Adventure Brothers and The Knights of Chivalry.

There had not been many serious challenges for us as partners. Everything had been easy. At two-thirty I shook Andrew's hand and boarded the shuttle bus alone. As my bus pulled out of the station, we drove right by McInnes. He was saluting me.

"Fare well, Adventure Brother," he shouted proudly, "Until we meet again!"

SIXTEEN

Welcome to New Zealand

My flight to Christchurch was quick, only three hours. I felt great. Recharged. I was experiencing the same sense of euphoric freedom that I had first felt upon arriving in Australia. You know, the finger-in-the-peanut-butter-thing.

It was a little after 8pm and as I walked the fifty yards from the plane to the terminal, I had my first brush with winter I'd had in a long time. When I'd left the States it was Fall — Southern California Fall. I had a nice tan. When I'd landed in Australia, Summer was just beginning. I'd cheated Mother Nature out of one winter, and it was time to put on a jacket.

"Holy shit, do I even have a jacket?"

When I entered the terminal, I was a little disappointed to see three long, slow-moving lines in front of me. I bitched under my breath and joined the shortest of the three lines, which happened to be the one on the right. I've always been one of those annoying people who asks those around him in line whether or not he's in the right line. This time, however, I thought about it before asking.

First of all, I wondered why there were three separate lines. And why was the one I chose the shortest? Was it shorter simply because fewer people had chosen it? Was the man checking passports at the front of this line simply faster than the two other passport checkers? Or was there another factor to which I was oblivious? I looked around at all the signs for a clue, but they just said things like "Please Have Your Passport Ready" and "Welcome to New Zealand" (I secretly scanned for a sign reading "ENTER THIS LINE ONLY IF IT IS YOUR BIRTHDAY). General stuff.

I decided not to ask anybody around me whether or not I was in the proper line, because that was what I would have done back when I was just a boy of twenty-six. Men don't ask other people whether they're in the right line or not. They simply find out at the front that they've been waiting in the wrong line and then say something like "Oh, my mistake. Silly me."

Instead, I turned to the man standing next to me in the middle line, which was to my left, and said,

"I hate waiting in line. Especially when it's my birthday."

"Me too," he said.

"It's your birthday too?" I asked, astonished.

"No. I just hate waiting on line."

He said "on" line. It seems that all other countries wait "on" line while we in America wait "in" line. I wondered about this. Perhaps it began in Eastern Europe where the citizens are forced to endure long lines while waiting for items such as bread and toilet paper. Maybe the authorities actually paint lines on the pavement to show them where they must stand. I'd hate to live in a place where I'd have to stand on line.

There was a middle-aged couple in front of me in line and they'd been listening as the man next to me and I spoke.

"Is today really your birthday?" asked the lady.

"Yes, it really is," I said proudly.

"Then you go ahead of us," said the man. Another lady in front of them did the same thing and I was passed all the way to the front of the line. As the only person in front of me was completing her business at the counter, I was smiling in thanks to the long line behind me, when a man near the back yelled to me,

"What's your name, mate?"

"Dave," I yelled back. He then surprised me by breaking out into a hearty and enthusiastic rendition of "Happy Birthday." Everybody in all three lines immediately joined in, and perhaps eighty people were singing to me after only minutes of my arrival in New Zealand.

"I think I'm really going to like this country!" I yelled to the smiling crowd when they'd finished. I was feeling pretty darn special as I stepped up to the Immigration counter. For about five seconds I stood there looking at the officer in front of me, and he at me. I began to wonder why he wasn't processing me or doing anything official. I thought that perhaps he was just offering me a moment of birthday respect before resuming official business.

Then I realized that I hadn't given him my passport. "Whoops, I'm sorry, you want my passport don't you?" I quickly dug it out of my zippered money belt and put it on the counter between us. I shook my head in mild disgust with myself because I'd read several signs urging me to have my passport ready and then I didn't have it ready. Oh well, at least I was in the right line. Or on it.

As soon as the man flipped my passport open to the page containing my name and photograph, his expression changed from one of boredom to one of near-terror. He immediately backed up two or three steps behind the counter as though he were trying to increase the distance between us and he raised my passport up in the air and began waving it frantically. Suddenly, uniformed officers converged on me from every direction and I found myself surrounded by a dozen policemen.

I glanced around at the ring of officers just to make sure that I was the one they were surrounding. I was the one, alright. Not only was I at the very center of their circle, but they were all staring at me as well.

"I didn't cut in line... they let me go to the front." An older, distinguished-looking gentleman in a tie stepped through the circle and faced me.

"Are you David Mulligan?"

"Yes."

"Come with me please." He started to turn away.

"It's about Cindy, isn't it? He faced me again.

"I beg your pardon?"

"Cindy. The stewardess on my plane. You're her husband, aren't you? I swear, she said she was single." Several people in the crowd laughed out loud. I suppose I was hoping for a chuckle from this man to break the tension, because I knew that whatever was happening was some kind of mistake. I realized as soon as I'd finished my little joke, however, that the police obviously felt that I was guilty of some serious crime and this was not the time for humor.

The man in the tie merely narrowed his eyes slightly and turned away from me again. The circle of uniformed officers parted to allow him through. I felt a firm push from the rear and I followed. As I was being led away, I heard a lady in the line behind me say to those around her,

"I wonder if today is really even his birthday?" I turned and said,

"No, it is. It really is my birthday." It was important to me that those people who'd been so kind as to sing to me know that I hadn't lied to them. It was clear that my public arrest had seriously affected my credibility.

"I assure you all," I continued over my shoulder as I was being taken away, "this is a mistake, and your kind gesture was not wasted on a criminal."

I was taken to a small room and deposited in a chair. The only chair. In fact, it was the only object in the room. The man in the tie stood at the open door holding my passport. An elderly uniformed officer entered with a small tape recorder in his hand. The man in the tie then closed the door behind him and the two of them faced me. The older gentleman then turned on the recorder.

"Mr. Mulligan," began the man in the tie, "we're going to record our conversation. Do you have any objection?" I shook my head.

"Does that mean 'No'?"

"Does what mean 'No'?" I asked.

"You just shook your head, didn't you?" I nodded.

"Alright, stop the tape Stephen." He looked irritated. "Mr. Mulligan, you seem to think this is a big bloody joke. It's not. You're in a heap of trouble. Now answer audibly and quit fucking about." Elderly Stephen then fumbled with the small buttons and managed to turn the recorder on again. It was apparent that the tiny machine was not a product of his generation and he was frustrated with it. The man in the tie began again. "Mr Mulligan, we're going to record this conversation. Do you have any..." At that moment, the small recorder began to play very loudly. The three of us jumped simultaneously. Through the speaker came the voice of a young boy, as Stephen tried in vain to turn off the machine.

" ... F is for fucker, G is for a Gail's big tits, H is for hell, I is for In your asshole, J is for..." Stephen, who was frantically searching for the stop button, found it and the tape stopped. His face and neck were dark red.

"I really wanted to hear what J was for," I said. The man in the tie was smiling at Stephen and the old man shook his head in embarrassment.

"Sorry. My son's boy was up for the weekend. I see the little bastard got into my desk." The tape recorder incident brought out the "human" in my interrogators, allowing them to loosen up a little bit and the man in the tie resumed his questioning on a much less serious plane.

It turned out that they had received a call earlier that day from Canberra, Australia's capital, notifying them that there was a man on the next flight into Christchurch who'd been thrown out of Australia. I was that man. The Christchurch officials were given my name and no other information; not even the reason for the disciplinary action. As far as the New Zealand officials were concerned, I could have been a terrorist. The large number of police officers were on hand just in case I was the sort of terrorist who got angry when I was deported.

My identity was being checked on computer about the same time as we were being graced by Stephen's grandson's recitation of the ABC's. Fewer than ten minutes later, my identity was confirmed and the New Zealand officials learned that the only reason I'd been ejected from Australia was that I had attempted to wait tables at Darwin's Atrium Hotel.

While this enlightenment got me off the hook in one respect, it put me right onto another hook. If I had sought employment in Australia, what would keep me from seeking employment in New Zealand? The man in the tie asked me that very question, and, while I should have been, I was not well prepared to answer it.

"Well, yes, I did try and get a job there. But I wouldn't do that here."

"Why not?"

"Well, any one of a number of reasons, really."

"Let's start with one."

"Okay. Because I came here for pleasure only." This was, of course, a lie. I planned on getting a job right away. I only had eighty dollars left and I was hoping with all of my being that he wouldn't ask me how much money I had.

"How much money do you have?" he asked.

"Oh, plenty."

"How much?" he pressed.

"Well, I've got some cash, and I've also got a credit card." This was true. In addition to my eighty dollars, I also possessed a Visa card which had expired over a year earlier. And even if it hadn't been expired, it would have been worthless because I'd maxed it out three weeks after receiving it and the Visa people were looking for me. I was hoping with all of my being that he wouldn't ask to see my credit card.

"May I see your credit card please? And the cash?"

"Of course." I unzipped my money belt and pulled out a crepe-thin fold of Australian notes and my less than worthless Visa card. New Zealand was as close as the door, yet I knew that was in grave danger of being sent home to America. If he noticed the expiration date, I'd be on the next plane. He counted the cash first.

"I count eighty Australian dollars. Not exactly a fortune."

"That's just pocket change," I said, with a casual chuckle. He handed me the cash and then turned his attention to my Visa card.

"What's your spending limit on this?" he asked.

"Three thousand dollars." This was, of course, a lie. The original limit had been one thousand dollars, and, as I said, I'd spent that in three weeks.

"And what's your current balance?"

"About a thousand dollars." This was a true statement. The last piece of hate mail I'd received from Visa before leaving the States said that I owed them nine hundred and forty dollars.

He examined my card closely. He turned it over and looked at my signature on the back. He then opened my passport and compared the signature there to the one on the back of the card. This caused me even more anxiety because the signature in my passport was not my own. My brother had signed it when he'd gone to pick up a document for me and discovered that I'd forgotten to sign my own passport. I sat silently in front of the man in the tie, knowing that the next thing to come out of his mouth would either be in regard to the dissimilar signatures or the date of expiration on my Visa card. Instead, he said,

"I advise you to be careful with this card. Before you know it, you'll be at your limit." And then he handed it to me. I let out a sigh of relief and unpuckered my sphincter. It was suddenly clear that I was going to be allowed into the country. However, the man in the tie evidently felt that I must be disciplined at least partially for being the cause of such a stir, so he allowed me to have only a one month entry visa instead of the normal ninety days. I opened my mouth to object, but I realized that I was pretty lucky to be staying at all, so I didn't say anything. Besides, I knew that I was going to stay for at least three months no matter what the stamp in my passport said. I'd worry about the legalities later.

I was released from custody just before ten p.m., and I almost missed the last bus into town. When the bus driver asked what my destination was, I told him "downtown, please."

"Cathedral Square?" he asked.

"That sounds fine" I said.

"That'll be a dollar, thanks."

"Do you accept Australian dollars? I had a bit of a hassle in there and I wasn't able to exchange my money."

"You're the one who was arrested, aren't you?"

"Well, I wasn't really arrested. They just questioned me because I got into a little trouble in Australia."

"I hope you don't mind my asking you this...," he said, "is today really your birthday? Everybody on the bus was arguing about it."

"Yes. It really is my birthday." He smiled broadly, exhibiting bad teeth. "Happy birthday, mate. There's no charge for you today. Welcome to New Zealand."

SEVENTEEN

A Kinder, Gentler Nation

A t ten-thirty I stood alone in the middle of Cathedral Square, eating from a steaming paper bag of fish and chips (which I'd doused in vinegar). The proprietor who'd supplied this meal had been kind enough to accept my Australian currency and had even exchanged a few extra dollars for me. The huge, sprawling square in which I stood was not well lit, but the massive cathedral at its edge was.

Flood lights illuminated the old stone structure all the way to peak of the spire, towering over a hundred and fifty feet above. I was drawn to the cathedral. I wanted to know how old it was; I wanted to climb an ancient, cobwebbed, spiral staircase up through its bowels and stand on the tiny balcony at its pinnacle.

Unfortunately, however, I found the front doors locked. This disappointed me. I'd expected it to be open because I thought all churches were open twenty-four hours a day. Like Seven-Eleven. What if I were a religious person experiencing a religious crisis? Where would I go? I then assumed that a religious person would know the business hours of the church and would find the strength to contain his or her religious crisis until the church opened in the morning.

Next, I needed to find a bed for the night. If I'd still been in Australia, in the warmer climate, I simply would have found a secluded patch of park-grass to make my bed, but Christchurch was a bit too nippy for that. On a fluke, really, I flipped through my address book and found something about which I'd forgotten.

A Kiwi friend of mine at home, a man by the name of Owen Rutledge, had given me his sister's name and number in Christchurch. Owen had grown up in Christchurch and left New Zealand at the age of twenty-one to see the world. That was sixteen years earlier and he'd never returned. The only description he'd given me of his sister, Helen, was that she was "quite nice" and had "bigger-than-average tits" (Owen could speak of virtually any subject and somehow bring breasts into the conversation). I knew nothing else about Helen; except, of course, her phone number.

I dropped a twenty-cent piece into a pay phone, dialed the six-digit number and listened to the foreign double-ring.

"Hello?" It was a friendly, female hello.

"Hi. I'm sorry to call so late," I said, stuttering slightly. "My name is Dave Mulligan. Is this Helen Rutledge?"

"I used to be Helen Rutledge; now I'm Helen Harper. May I help you?"

"Yes. Well, maybe. I've just arrived in the country, and Owen gave me your number..." She spoke up instantly, her voice full of joy and exuberance.

"You know Owen?"

"Yes. Owen's a good friend of mine. We drink beer together."

"Where did you see him?"

"We're neighbors. I'm from Redondo Beach, in America, where Owen lives."

"Are you in Christchurch?" she asked.

"Yes. I'm standing in Cathedral Square." It was at this point when I began to feel a little awkward because it would soon become obvious, if it hadn't already, that I needed a place to stay.

"Great! We'll have to meet some time. Where are you staying?"

"Well, I just arrived, and I haven't gone to a hotel yet...."

"Oh, that's wonderful! You'll stay with us!"

"I couldn't... it's so late... "

"Don't be silly! I'll come and pick you up. You say you're in the Square?

"Yes. At the pay phones."

"You stay right where you are, I'll be there in ten minutes. Look for an old Triumph."

After hanging up, I stood there in the phone booth for a few moments, amazed at what a kind, warm person Helen Harper was. It was almost eleven o'clock at night, I was a complete stranger, and she was rushing right over to pick me up. What luck. And I didn't even have to tell her that it was my birthday.

Ten minutes hadn't elapsed when Helen Harper pulled up in her old Triumph sedan. Physically, she was not at all what I expected. I'd expected a sister-type, perhaps because Owen had seen reason to include her breasts in his description of her. She was the mom-type, however. Fortyish. Plain, soft, cuddly, warm. Rosy cheeks, big sweater, a touch of grey at the temples. A bit worn on the edges from years of providing love and sacrifice. Definitely a mom. She greeted me with a warm and enthusiastic hug and then opened the trunk, or "boot," for me to stow my backpack.

When we were seated in the car, I apologized again for calling so late and I explained to her the circumstances which had led to my earlier-than-expected departure from Australia which had led, in turn, to my earlier-than-expected arrival in New Zealand.

Helen was a great lady. It didn't seem to bother her in the least that I'd called so late and had shown up completely unannounced. She claimed that she was up until midnight every night anyway, cleaning up after her husband and four sons. She was kind and polite and expressed an interest in the story of my travels, but it was clear to me that what she wanted to talk about most was her brother Owen.

I could see that she loved him and missed him dearly, so, as she drove, I did my very best to share with her all I knew about her younger brother. I told her how Owen and I had met, how we'd hit it off well and become regular drinking buddies and of Owen's legendary womanizing. (I did not tell her, however, that the last time I'd gone drinking with her brother he'd thrown up on a telephone pole next to a busy highway and was later arrested for drunk driving.) Helen was delighted by every detail in my recollections. This was as close as she'd been able to come to her brother in years and she was overjoyed to get a first-hand account of his life in the United States.

When we arrived at the Harper house, I expected the family to be in bed. However, all were up and, judging by their behavior, it was clear that Helen had instructed them to greet me upon my arrival. There were four sons in all, ranging from nine to eighteen. Allistaire, the youngest, was shy, courteous, and lovable. As soon as he got over his initial fear of me, he began asking me everything I knew about American pro wrestling. Kallum, 13, was a bit soft, freckled, had braces, was polite enough, but was somewhat distracted because he was 13. Dylan, 15, was also dutifully polite, yet played the tough guy, maintaining a chest-out posture throughout our introduction. Ryan was the eldest at 18 and was extremely polite and pleasant. He was tall, with dark, curly hair like his Uncle Owen and an innocent smile, unlike his Uncle Owen.

No more than ten minutes after the four boys had said their obligatory "hellos," Paul, Helen's husband, sent them curtly to bed. I suppose it's rather common, yet it's always surprising anyway, to meet a warm, marvelous person, like Helen, who's matched up with a partner who does not possess the same endearing qualities. The old saying is true; opposites attract. This is not to say that Paul Harper was an asshole; he was simply the opposite of warm and marvelous.

He was a young, handsome, New Zealand version of Archie Bunker, complete with his own chair/throne in the family room and an attitude toward his wife and sons which said "Dingbat" and "Meathead." He was allowing me to stay under his roof, however, and for this I was certainly grateful.

Roughly thirty minutes after the boys had been sent to bed, Allistaire, the youngest, appeared in the living room in his pajamas, rubbing his eyes.

"I'm sorry, Dad, I'm thirsty... is it okay if I get a drink of water." Paul glared at his young son.

"Dammit, boy. Why aren't you smart enough to get a drink before bed?" he yelled. Little Allistaire looked scared and embarrassed. Helen stepped in and did her best to remedy the awkward situation. It was clear to me that she, too, was embarrassed by Paul's treatment of Allistaire. When she'd finished helping her son, I announced that it was time for me to be getting to bed. I said goodnight and thanked Paul, then Helen showed me to the guest room.

I thanked her profusely for her hospitality and she assured me that it was her pleasure to have me there and that I was welcome to stay as long as I liked. As soon as I'd gotten into bed and quit moving, I heard faint crying coming through the wall from Kallum and Allistaire's room next door. It was young Allistaire. Poor little guy. I felt sad for him because he'd never know what it was like to be loved by a father like I'd been by mine.

A memory surfaced that I hadn't thought about for years. My father moved our family out from Maryland to Southern California when I was six years old. I was in the first grade and it was the middle of the school year when we made the move. In retrospect, I'm sure that my father understood how traumatic it can be for a kid to change schools, especially in the middle of the year, but he'd just gotten a new job on a television show and he had no choice.

My little sister wasn't starting school yet and my big brother was old enough to handle the move alright. But for me, it was terrifying. My new school was only a block from our new house and on my first day, my dad walked me over and brought me to the office where I was registered and introduced me to the principal. His name was Mr. Lightbody. I was scared of him and everybody else in the office and I don't think I said a word. Soon it was time for me to be taken to my homeroom.

As Mr. Lightbody led us down the hall, I held my dad's hand tightly. As we drew closer, I finally succumbed to my anxiety and began to cry. Mr. Lightbody began to say something about how there was nothing to worry about and my father cut in and asked if he could stay with me for a little while before I went into class. The principal, I recall, seemed a little uneasy with this, but agreed and left us alone sitting on a bench. I was terrified of entering the room full of complete strangers and I couldn't imagine what it would be like without my dad there.

I probably cried for half an hour as he held my hand on that bench. I remember him saying to me that, even after he left, his love would still be with me. He'd love me all day long from wherever he was, so I should never feel alone or scared.

"But please don't leave me yet," I pleaded.

"I won't leave until you're ready," he assured me. My father and I went through this same routine on that little bench for my whole first week at my new school. The crying period grew shorter each day until I'd adjusted. Through all of the terrible fear and anxiety I'd felt, my dad never left my side before I was ready.

And that's the sort of father he remained until I was twenty-four; when he left long before I was ready. I don't know how long Helen had been tapping on the door before I woke up and realized where I was and figured out what the sound was.

"Good morning," I said as cheerily as possible in my half-conscious state.

"Good morning. Are you presentable?"

"Yes, sure. C'mon in."

"I hope you slept alright," she said, entering. "That old bed sags in the middle."

"It was a great night's sleep. I don't think I moved once all night. What time is it?"

"Half past eight. I was going to let you sleep on, but I thought you might want to come along with us to Ryan's rugby match."

She'd mentioned Ryan's game to me just before I'd gone to bed, and my weariness may have concealed my enthusiasm. I was glad she was giving me another opportunity.

"Yeah, thanks, I'd love to go!"

"Good. Come have some breakfast."

"Is everyone going?"

"All but Paul. He's working." I was more than slightly relieved to hear that Paul was not in the house and would not be joining us. I found him rather intimidating and felt as though he didn't entirely welcome me.

"Okay," I said, "I'll be right out." I said this with a quick nod and a half-smile. This is the universal gesture which means "I'm naked under this blanket and I can't stand up until you leave the room." Helen caught on immediately and gave the proper response, which is a half-smile accompanied by a wink, and ducked out.

Standing on the sideline of Ryan's rugby game with the rest of the Harpers (except for Paul, of course) and scores of other spectators, I could not have been more content; except, perhaps, if I were actually out there on the field myself. I was eighteen years old before I'd ever even heard of the game of rugby. It was on my very first day at college, at the University of Oregon, when I walked into my dorm room to meet my new roommate.

I had a black eye and carried a case of Ranier 16 ounce beers on my shoulder. My roommate, a burly-looking sophomore named Condos, shook my hand and asked me if I'd ever considered playing rugby.

"What's rugby?" I asked him.

"Come out to practice tonight and I'll show you," he said. He did and my life would never be the same. Rugby is as much a way of life as it is a sport; that is, it continues off the field and permeates one's life even when one is not carrying the ball or wearing one's jersey. There is commonly as much action in a rugby team's favorite bar as may be witnessed on the field in Saturday's game. This "zest for life" common to rugby players does not manifest itself in the form of violence in the bar, though.

No, the hitting ends when the ref blows the final whistle. You will, however, see drinking like you've never seen before and hear belching which borders on the violent. An hour or so into the party, the singing will begin.

These are songs which no mother should hear; due to the fact that many are about mothers... or daughters, nuns, Girl

Scouts, etc. At two hours into the rugby party, all self-respecting, self-preserving females should be out of the building. Every rugby party ends differently, but the best exit I ever witnessed was the "Parade of the Flaming Assholes." An entire team, buck naked, marched out of a bar, single file, each man with a rolled-up, flaming newspaper protruding from his ass. Rugby. Being a part of it again made me grin as I stood and watched Ryan Harpers game in what is arguably the rugby capital of the world.

Well into the second half of Ryan's game, a fellow of about my age approached me and introduced himself. He'd noticed my accent, it seemed, and was curious about me. He was surprised when I told him that I played rugby in the United States; he'd been under the impression that the only sports we played in America were football, baseball, basketball, and professional wrestling (this wrestling thing was beginning to bother me. He was the third Kiwi to bring it up after finding out that I was American. I found it very disturbing that some of America's most prominent representatives around the world were intellectual giants like Hulk Hogan).

He then told me that he played for the Christchurch rugby club and asked me if I'd be interested in playing for them. Of course, I only planned on being in Christchurch for about a week, though, so I had to turn him down. It did feel good to be asked and it made me seriously consider hooking up with a club once I got down to Queenstown.

Over the next few days I spent quite a bit of time with Helen and the Harper boys. I was grateful for the fact that Paul was such a hard-working man, because this meant that he was almost always at work. I appreciated every moment with Helen and her sons and I couldn't imagine any better way to learn about a foreign country than by living with a family.

I ate what they ate (a lot of hearty, "meat and potatoes" type meals, and the freshest, creamiest milk I've ever had), I played touch rugby with the boys in the back yard (every kid in New Zealand grows up playing rugby, so even Allistaire, at ten, could pass the ball better than I), I watched the same T.V. shows they did (the Harper brothers' favorite show was, to my great horror, American W.W.F. wrestling. I cannot tell you how depressing it was for me to see Hulk Hogan flexing spasmodically while foaming at the mouth and screaming at me as if I'd never left home).

After one week of hanging out with the Harper brothers, who all happened to be on break from their respective schools, I felt like I was beginning to get the hang of New Zealand. On the following Monday, the boys were all back in school, Helen was at her part-time job and I was the only one at the house. I decided to hitch-hike into town to walk around and see the sights.

I'd been into town several times (one trip included a tour of the magnificent cathedral, which didn't disappoint me), either with Helen or the boys, or both, but I'd never been into town by myself. I just wanted to walk around, take things in, have a beer and maybe meet a girl. I only had a couple of days before I was going to stuff my backpack and head up to Queenstown to meet McInnes, so I wanted to experience as much of Christchurch as I could before leaving. I visited several pubs. One could stand in front of any pub in downtown Christchurch and be only an empty can's throw from the next pub. They were literally on every corner and every one was uniquely charming.

The fourth or fifth bar I visited was in an old, restored, converted hotel. The "Occidental." Actually, I discovered two bars when I entered the old hotel; one to the right, and the other to the left. I peeked in through the engraved glass doors of the one on the right first, "Chat's," and saw that it was inhabited by three snifter-sipping elderly men sporting jackets and ties. I quickly decided that it was a bit quiet for my current mood. Beautiful though.

Opposite Chat's was "Perry's." While almost devoid of customers due to the post-lunch, pre-happy-hour time of the day, Perry's still struck me immediately as my kind of place, with plenty of space, a big, rectangular "Cheers" style bar jutting right out into the middle of the room, twenty or thirty tables scattered about on dark maroon carpet, old photos on the walls and a stage occupied by a covered key board and sound equipment. I could smell and feel the dormant fun in the room.

The few customers in Perry's sat scattered about at the tables and one man at the bar itself. I figured that only lonely people who wish to remain lonely will sit alone at a table, so I moved directly to the bar and mounted a stool.

"Hello sir, what pleases you?" asked the bartender, a middle-aged man with a grey beard, thick glasses, and a leaning bow tie.

"Beer pleases me, thank you."

"Do you have a preference?"

"Actually, I haven't been in the country long enough to develop a preference."

"I see," he said, empathetically.

"Why don't you pour me what you would drink," I asked.

"That would be a scotch."

"No, I don't want that. Just pour me a big glass of the average, working man's beer."

"Well, you're in luck. It just so happens that my friend Rex here is the average working man. Isn't that right, Rex?" Rex was fortyish, reasonably well-dressed in a v-neck sweater over a shirt and tie and was rather tired-looking.

"I used to be. Now I'm older than the average working man." After hearing these few words from Rex I was able to deduce that he was not merely tired, but slightly intoxicated.

"Tell this young Canadian gentleman, Rex, which beer you drink as a slightly older than average working man."

"Very well. I drink DB."

"Well, there you have it, sir. Would you care to try a DB?"

"I'd love a DB, please. And, by the way, I'm American, not Canadian."

"Oh, sorry mate. It's just that we get a lot more Canadians through here than Americans and I can't tell your accents apart."

"That's alright, I can't tell your accent from an Australian one either." This was true. They were identical to my ear.

"You're joking mate. We don't sound at all alike." Sounding to me exactly like an Australian, he said this as he pulled a large tap handle and began filling my glass with a beautiful amber beer.

"What's your name, friend?" he asked as he placed my beer on a cardboard coaster in front of me on the bar.

"I'm Mulligan." What's yours?"

"They call me Soggy, Mulligan. It's a pleasure to meet you. " We shook hands before I asked him the obvious question.

"Soggy'? Is that the name your parents gave you? Or is it a nickname?"

"Actually, my doctor gave me that name. I went to see him one day when I used to drink quite a bit and, after he examined me, he told me that my liver was soggy with alcohol. It's been my name ever since." I raised my glass in a toast. "Well, gentlemen, here's to DB, the average working man,

Soggy's liver and New Zealand!" Soggy produced a short glass of scotch from behind the bar, he and I clinked glasses,

Rex lifted his DB at the other end of the bar and the three of us took a drink.

As happy hour neared, the bar slowly began to fill with an attractive, yuppie clientele. At five minutes before five, Soggy's bar phone rang and he picked it up. He listened for a few moments before his jovial expression turned to one of frustration, then of anger, and then he simply said,

"Well I guess that's that then" and hung up.

"Is everything alright?" I asked. I felt that I was not out of bounds for asking him this because I had raised a glass with him and I knew the story of his nickname, so I was just close enough to Soggy to pry slightly into his business.

"No it isn't, really. That was Diane, my boss upstairs. The bastard who's supposed to relieve me at five called Diane and to tell her that he can't make it. This is about the tenth time he's done this, so she sacked him. This means that I have to stay on till closing. I've been here since bloody ten this morning!"

"Hey listen," I said. "I'm a pretty good bartender. Maybe your boss will let me work for you? I could use the money ..." The opportunity seemed too good for me to resist. Besides, it was true that I needed the money. I was down to less than thirty dollars.

"It couldn't hurt to ask her, could it, Mulligan? She's got to replace that lazy bastard anyway. You say you've worked behind a bar before?"

"Yes. I've worked in a few bars." This was true. It had been a couple of years, but it's not rocket science. Soggy picked up the phone and called his boss. Diane appeared behind the bar almost immediately following her brief phone conversation with Soggy (which I'd tried to hear, but Soggy had spoken too quietly. I hoped that he'd given me a good recommendation).

She was big, blonde, and pretty. I've rarely described a woman as "handsome," but the adjective fit her. She was at least six feet tall and exceptionally curvacious, with thick, shiny blonde hair pulled back in a ponytail. She had bright green eyes and plump, ripe, sexy lips which she accentuated with brilliant red lipstick. She was dressed conservatively in a long navy skirt, and a long-sleeved, white blouse, buttoned up to her throat.

She introduced herself with an assertive handshake and asked me to follow her over to Chat's where it was much quieter. She led me to a booth next to a window facing the street and we sat across from one another.

"Clarence tells me that you're looking for work."

"Clarence?"

"Yes. Oh, you probably know him as 'Soggy'."

"Yeah. Now I know why he uses a nickname." She chuckled. "I assume he told you that I had to terminate another barman tonight..."

"Yes, he did. I love tending bar and I told him that I'd work for him tonight if he couldn't get anybody to cover his shift."

"Have you worked behind a bar before?"

"Sure. Several times."

"Are you looking for permanent work."

"Actually, I'm leaving town in a couple of days. I just wanted to make a few dollars before I move on."

"He tells me you're American. Do you have a work visa?"

This was bound to come up.

"Not with me." I said. She nodded and grinned knowingly.

"I see. Well, I'll get you a shirt and a bow tie. Your jeans will have to do for tonight. Normally the barmen wear black pants. I'll have Clarence stay on until happy hour ends at seven. Most of the customers leave then, so you shouldn't have too much trouble. It'll be slow. The pay is nine dollars an hour. It doubles after midnight, but you'll be closing by eleven. I'll be upstairs in my apartment, so you can ring me if there's a rush and you need help. I'm sure it will take me a couple of days to fill the position, would you like to work tomorrow and Thursday night too?" No more than ten minutes later, I stood behind the bar with Soggy, wearing a fresh white shirt and a black bow tie.

I called Helen and told her that I was working late and would miss dinner. She was impressed.

EIGHTEEN

The Relapse

Soggy stayed with me for the first hour of my shift in Perry's and showed me where everything was. It was Tuesday, one of the three nights during the week when Dwayne, a singer/comedian, was not on stage doing his show, so there were less than twenty customers in the bar after the happy hour crowd evacuated at seven. Soggy explained that it was probably a good thing that I was starting on a Tuesday night, because the nights when Dwayne was on stage, Perry's was packed.

I needed a slow night to get the hang of things; like which glass I was supposed to use for which drink, how to operate the cash register, etc. One of the most frustrating parts for me was familiarizing myself with the New Zealand money. It had taken me weeks to get used to the Australian currency, to be able to recognize a coin or bill at a glance. The Kiwi money was completely different and represented a whole new challenge.

My awkward performance at the cash register didn't seem to bother any of the customers, though. In fact, they found it rather amusing. Even more challenging for me were the drinks themselves. For instance, two young businessmen in loosened ties strode in and sat at my bar, and the one on the left said,

"Let us have two bourbons, mate."

"Sure. How would you like them?" I asked, sincerely puzzled. They looked at one another, smiling. The one on the right then said,

"Oh, in a glass of some sort would be nice, I suppose."

"What I meant was, would you like your bourbon on the rocks, or in a shot glass, or what? You'll have to be more specific with me because I'm new here and I really don't know what the hell I'm doing yet." As it turned out, they wanted two bourbon-and-cokes. In Christchurch, New Zealand, I had just learned, if one merely said "bourbon" to the bartender, he or she would expect to be handed a bourbon-and-coke.

A well-dressed woman in her forties then appeared at the bar and requested a glass of white wine. Feeling very unsure of myself, I asked her,

"Just on its own?" She chuckled and said,

"Well, if you're afraid it'll get lonely, give me two so they can keep each other company." In any new job, I reminded myself, there will be a period of time when the new employee will inevitably make an asshole out of his or her self, either in front of customers, or in front of fellow employees. This humiliation can be handled in one of two ways; the perpetrator may turn red, hang his or her head in embarrassment, go about his or her business and appear pitiful to all who have witnessed the faux pas; or, he or she may choose to laugh out loud, turn and meet the look of all who watch and say, quite loudly, something to the effect of "Boy, only an asshole would do something like that, eh?" I chose to use the "Boy, only an asshole" method, sharing in my own teasing and effectively neutralizing my ridicule.

Diane, my kind, Amazonian boss, appeared now and then during my first shift in Perry's and, at the end of the night, asked me if I'd be interested in working five nights a week. She said that I'd impressed her with the way I dealt with customers. I opened my mouth to explain to her my plans to meet Andrew in Queenstown, but, instead, I heard myself say,

"I'd love to." It was an opportunity too good to pass up and I was sure that McInnes would understand. I would try and reach him by phone somehow in Queenstown on the day of our planned rendezvous and I hoped that there would be a listing in the yellow pages for "Bungee Jumping."

I awoke the next morning feeling employed and secure, and I knew that, since I had decided to stay in Christchurch for a while, it was time for me to move out of the Harpers' and find my own place. I was happy with myself for sprouting wings so quickly and I was eager to leave the nest. Helen drove me into town after breakfast and dropped me off at a boarding house just around the corner from Cathedral Square.

She'd had friends and relatives stay there several times and she insisted it was the nicest boarding house in town. I vowed to Helen that I'd stay in touch and I meant it. There was no doubt in my mind that I would. Certainly, there were people I'd met along my travels with whom I'd exchanged addresses with no intention of contacting ever again, but Helen was not one of those. She had been more than generous to me and had also become a good friend. She made me promise that I would visit them once a week for dinner and then she drove off.

Like the Oxy, the boarding house where I decided to make my temporary home was only about five minutes' walk from Cathedral Square. It was an old, three-storey, brick affair (for some reason, all brick buildings are referred to as "brick affairs") with wooden floors and squeaky stairs. Most of the thirty rooms contained New Zealanders who were either just passing through, down on their luck, or too odd to get a normal place of their own; but the building also housed several international travelers like myself. I had my own little room on the third floor overlooking a small park.

My room contained a garage-sale chest of drawers; an exhausted, leaning armoire; a peeling, two-foot square table which passed for a writing desk; an accompanying, equally deteriorated chair; and a sagging cot which, like the stairs, squeaked and complained under my weight. But, as dilapidated as my room and its contents appeared to be, it was clean and charming and was the first room of my own I'd had since leaving home. I hadn't realized just how much I missed simple privacy until I entered my little room for the first time and closed the door behind me.

Christchurch, I soon learned, was a drinking town. With a ratio of about three pubs for every two citizens, there was certainly no shortage of places to find a cold beer and a friendly face and the Occidental was just about the most popular spot in town. It took me less than a week to feel right at home at the Oxy; it was like a big party in there on the busy nights and, as bartender, I found myself right in the middle of the action.

When crowd size demanded, there would be two, or even three, of us pouring drinks and, often, we would face a thirsty, undulating mob standing four-deep at the bar. I can't honestly say that I got good fast, but I did get fast fast. It was a situation where there simply was not a choice. Supply had to meet demand, and I was the supplier.

The day when I was supposed to meet McInnes in Queenstown at the bungee jumping bridge had come and gone, and I could find no way of reaching him and telling him of my change in plans. I felt guilty for abandoning him; I envisioned him standing there, politely stopping passers-by, "Excuse me, sir, I'm Andrew McInnes from Scotland. I was to meet an American here, my Adventure Brother and fellow Knight of Chivalry. Goes by the name of Mulligan. You haven't seen him, by chance, have you?"

I posted notes to him at all of the obvious points in town — the bus station, public bulletin boards, the front desk of my boarding house, etc. — in the hopes that he may come looking for me. He knew that I landed in Christchurch, so I felt that there was a chance he might show up. I hoped he would.

Since I had decided not to leave Christchurch, I accepted the offer of the rugby player I had met at Ryan Harper's game and joined the Christchurch rugby club. The club actually fielded six or seven teams; the very best athletes playing for the first side, the next best on the second side, and so on. As players got older or became less intense about the game, developed debilitating injuries, or got married, they slipped down the ladder to the next level of play where they would be more comfortable and less would be expected of them.

I chose to play for the third side because that was where I best fit and also because I would still be allowed to play in the Saturday afternoon games even if I were to miss the Thursday night training session (which I would have to miss most weeks because of work).

Playing rugby in New Zealand is something that all rugby players dream of doing, because it is widely felt that the Kiwis play the best rugby in the world. The "All Blacks," New Zealand's national side, have reigned supreme in the sport for as long as most "ruggers" can remember. My playing there was the equivalent of an ice hockey player visiting and playing in Canada, or a ping pong player getting a game in China (it is a little-known fact that a Mr. Ping, a Mr. Pong, and a Mr. Pang invented the game centuries ago, improvising with hand-held fans as paddles and an over-puffed grain of rice for a ball. The three were inseparable, the story goes, and they played day and night on a triangular table.

One evening at dinner, however, Mr. Pang, in a rush to get back to the game, choked on an under-chewed ball of sweet-and-sour pork and died. The rest of the story is obvious).

My first game with the Christchurch Rugby Club was a little bit of a let down for me. For days leading up to the match, I had fantasized about playing so well that old men, former players, watching on the sidelines would mutter things like, "Say, that American can really play," or "Plays a bit like I used to, that American lad." But, alas, I wasn't the star of the game.

In fact, I struggled just to manage to do my basic duties on the field. I wasn't in sync with the rhythm of the game. I was physically fit, I'd been running five miles almost every day, but there was something subtly different about the way the New Zealanders played the game which left me frustrated and feeling like I was chasing ghosts.

It seemed that every time I'd go to tackle a ball carrier, he'd pass the ball off to a teammate the instant before I'd hit him. Supporting one another and being there to receive a pass when a teammate is being tackled is a fundamental part of the game and one that I always understood, but these Kiwis did it so naturally and with such fluidity that I felt like a real novice. The fact that New Zealanders begin to play rugby as soon as they can walk was certainly apparent in the quality of their play and trying to adjust to their game was a real learning experience for me. I kept at it, though, and I improved with every game.

Several factors, including the fact that I was playing rugby and associating with rugby players, contributed to what I refer to as my "relapse," but the main reason I slipped and sank into the depths of Hell was the simple fact that I had become a bartender. This occupation will invariably place the subject in very close proximity to both alcohol and receptive females; and, unfortunately, I possessed a weakness for and an inclination to indulge in, both.

I had recently vowed, as I have outlined, to approach both alcohol and receptive females with moderation in mind. I had decided that I would pursue a girl romantically only if I found her to be extraordinarily attractive, both inside and out; and that I would drink in excess only if there were some special cause for celebration.

The first girl, I truly felt, was extraordinarily attractive, both inside and out, and, therefore, legally pursuable if I were to live by my freshly-penned, self-imposed, code of ethics. She was fair game. This grand occasion was certainly a cause for celebration, so, again living by the letter of my own new moral standards, I allowed myself the luxury of enjoying several drinks with this young beauty before proceeding any further.

The second girl was so extraordinarily attractive on the outside that the fact that she was a little less shiny on the inside became not so important. Inside and out balanced, therefore making her legal companionship by my new code. This, of course, was an occasion worthy of celebration and we drank four bottles of cheap champagne in the park.

The third girl was not extraordinarily attractive, but was rather pretty. She was not especially nice, and was a little on the simple side, but, as I said, she was rather pretty. While I can't honestly say that our union was an occasion worthy of great celebration, it was her seventeenth birthday, so we drank a bottle of bourbon in my room.

After that, I faded into a living, flesh-colored collage where, as I try to recollect, faces of varying beauty float independently above bodies of various sizes and shapes.

Slowly, and unintentionally, I turned my back on the code of ethics I had developed for myself, and I listened more and more to the little voice in my head.

In fact, I'm sure that there were many nights when I stayed at home in my room and my little voice went to work at the Oxy for me. I quickly developed a reputation which was even worse that the one I had tried so hard to overcome back at home. One of my nicknames was "Dirty Dave." All those months of growth, all the forward steps I had taken, all the advancements I had made toward becoming a man... wasted.

NINETEEN

Sophie

I t was a cold and rainy Tuesday in Christchurch, and I didn't feel like being at work. There were six people in the bar when I arrived to relieve Soggy, and, one hour later, there were four.

In the far corner of the room, at a small table in front of the glowing fireplace, sat two blurry figures. At the bar, right in front of me, sat a seventeen year-old gal and her eighteen-year old, gum-chomping best friend. Neither of them knew it for sure, but I had slept with both of them (perhaps I should add here, for my own protection, that the legal age in New Zealand for girls to choose with whom they will be intimate is sixteen).

They were quite suspicious of one another and neither would get up to use the ladies' room for fear of leaving me alone with the other one. I sat and listened to them as they giggled and chomped their bubble gum and felt as though they had been sent to punish me for becoming the letch that I was. They were physical examples of what my life had become, so I deserved to have to stand in their presence as they contemplated life's great mysteries.

One of the two blurry bodies from the corner table appeared at the bar, so I excused myself from my two giggling guests to help her. She was a plump woman of about forty-five and I thought I detected an English accent,

"I'd like two hot ports for us, please," she declared.

"Hot ports?" I asked, genuinely baffled.

"Yes," she said, coldly. "Port wine, heated."

"If you'll just guide me through this, I'll give you whatever you like," I said. This was my standard response when a customer ordered something with which I was unfamiliar (unless the bar was packed, then I'd simply hand them a DB).

"Alright," she said. "The port is right behind you there in the dark bottle with the red label. Yes, that one. Now, have you a microwave in the kitchen?"

"Sure."

"That'll do fine. Just fill two wine glasses with the port and warm them in your microwave for perhaps 15 seconds."

"That's simple enough," I said. "Why don't you go sit back down with your friend and I'll bring them over when they're ready." Although I found this woman to be cold and unfriendly, I offered to deliver the drinks so that I may enjoy a few moments of respite from the girls at the bar.

As I approached the table, a pleasantly warm and aromatic glass of port in each hand, I saw for the first time the English woman's companion. My first thought upon seeing her was "how in the hell did she get in here without my seeing her?" She was breathtaking; not tall and gorgeous like a cover girl, but warmer, softer, natural and serene. She had smooth, fair skin; pale, blue green eyes; blonde, shoulder-length hair alive with curls and character; and a set of matching dimples which pushed me over the edge. She was the only girl I'd ever seen whom I would have described as truly "radiant;" she glowed more brilliantly than the fire at her back.

I didn't know then, but I realized later, that I stood there for several seconds — a full wine glass in each hand —and stared at her. Her friend spoke and released me from my trance.

"Thank you, barman. Just set them down, if you would. Oh Sophie, doesn't the port smell heavenly!" Sophie's eyes twinkled and her dimples deepened as she smiled with excitement. "Oh yes, it smells lovely!" She, too, spoke with an accent, but it wasn't English. I couldn't place it. I knew that I should put the glasses down at that point and return to my position behind the bar, but I wanted Sophie to acknowledge my presence; I needed to see in her eyes that she saw me. I had the strongest sensation that my heart wouldn't beat again until Sophie looked at me and I became real and alive in her eyes. I spoke, only to Sophie.

"I wasn't sure how hot you wanted it... is it hot enough... or maybe too hot?" I put the glasses on the table.

Sophie looked at me and smiled benevolently, gently lifting the wine glass with both hands. She then put it to her lips and took a small, cautious sip. The warm smile returned, and then broadened as she looked up at me. "It's beautiful," she said; and I was in love with her.

I had to concentrate on how to walk as I weaved through several empty tables on my way back to the bar. There was no rhythm in my legs. Left, right, Sophie, left, Sophie, right, Sophie, Sophie. It was a long journey, a short trip, an instant, an eternity... and then I stood behind the bar again, eighteen inches from the Bimbos from Hell. I faced them, and suddenly they looked like two ridiculous wooden-headed puppets being operated by someone crouched between their stools.

I didn't hate them as much as I hated myself.

"What time will you be off shift?" asked the one on the right, arousing a nasty look from the one on the left.

"I should be out of here by twelve. My wife is flying in from America tomorrow morning, so I've got to get to sleep as early as I can." Their simultaneous expressions of shock, combined with their efforts to conceal any reaction at all from one another, almost made me laugh.

"Oh, I never knew you were married." said the one on the left.

"Neither did I," said the one on the right. "How come you don't wear a wedding ring?"

"Well," I said, looking from side to side, making certain that no one else was within earshot, "I used to wear it all the time, but last week a hooker stole it from me."

As my two acquaintances left the bar on heated feet only a few minutes later, I said to myself , "What timing... The girl I've always wanted just walked into my life, and here I am at my very sleaziest." I felt that I wasn't even worthy of looking at Sophie, let alone entertaining any thoughts of asking her for a date.

To approach her, I felt, would be to insult her. She was infinitely better than I. She was of another world, a clean world where people always knew their partner's name when they had sex. Actually, I pointed out to myself, Sophie and her sort didn't "have sex," they only *made love*.

Over the next half-hour, I made several passes through and around the corner of the bar where sat the incredibly lovely Sophie. I wiped the same table tops five times. I moved chairs to places they didn't belong, and then returned them. For the first time in my life, I dusted. Twice I tended to the fire; it was a gas fireplace with a ceramic log which required no tending. All of this I did to get closer to Sophie, to glimpse again those soft green eyes, those heavenly dimples.

Although I had vowed to myself that I would not approach her or interrupt their conversation, I could not resist.

"Excuse me for interrupting, but I've been trying to figure out your accent and I just can't. Do you mind if I ask where you're from?"

"I don't mind at all," she said, smiling again and activating her dimples. "I'm from Northern Ireland, near Belfast. And you're American, aren't you?"

"Yes. Was it my accent that gave me away, or the rude way I interrupted your conversation?" Sophie's friend, who had to remain consistent with the way she'd treated me so far, answered before Sophie could.

"Actually, we would rather prefer to be left alone to talk, if you don't mind."

"I'm sorry, I didn't mean to bother you ..." My eyes met Sophie's for an instant before I turned away and I saw pity in them. I was embarrassed, and she knew it. I limped back to the bar to pout.

Diane appeared a few moments later and told me to close the bar as soon as the two female guests in the corner finished their drinks. It was too slow to remain open, she said. I decided that I would not inform Sophie and her partner that we were going to close, I would, instead, allow them to finish their drinks and stay as long as they liked.

To my dismay, however, I looked over at Sophie and saw that she and her friend were standing and putting on their coats. Quickly, and completely without premeditation, I picked up a pen and wrote on the back of a cardboard beer coaster: "Sophie - My name is Dave Mulligan. For the past few months I've been living like somebody you wouldn't like. I haven't even liked myself. You would make me so happy if you'd allow me the opportunity of meeting you. Just speaking to you briefly has made me want to be who I was again. I work here every evening except Sunday. Please stop in and talk to me. You've cast a spell on me. Dave."

I hurried out from behind the bar and caught up to Sophie as she and her friend neared the door. She saw me and spoke before I could.

"Oh, there you are. We're just leaving. Thank you for the port, it was nice." I was nervous as hell, and I said,

"Here, this is for you" as I handed her the coaster, which was crudely folded in half. I hadn't planned on what was supposed to happen next, so I just stood there like an asshole with absolutely no expression and no Idea of what I should say.

She opened the coaster, turned it over because it was upside-down, and began reading. After a few moments of unbearable discomfort on my part, Sophie lifted her eyes from the note and smiled warmly at me. She was blushing.

"Thank you, Dave Mulligan, you're a sweet man." She then put my note in her coat pocket, and the two of them left.

I worked the next four nights and each time a body entered the bar, I was disappointed when I saw that it was not Sophie. The fifth night was Sunday, my day off. I had mentioned in my note to her that I had Sundays off, but I sat in the bar anyway in case she might show up. She didn't. I asked everybody I knew and people I'd never met if they knew Sophie. Nobody had ever heard of her. For the entire week, I drank very little because I wanted to be sharp and alert if she came in and I shared my bed with no one. As silly as the concept was, I felt that if I were to sleep with someone else, I would be cheating on Sophie.

Monday night found me back at work and when Sophie made no appearance, I accepted the fact that I would never see her again. Meeting her had been good for me, I decided, because our brief encounter allowed me to glimpse myself through decent eyes and I knew that I would never let myself sink that low again. I closed the bar at eleven, made the three-block walk to Cathedral Square where I turned right and walked three blocks to my boarding house and was in bed by eleven-thirty.

At twelve there was a tap at my door,

"Who is it?" I asked from my bed.

"Open the door and see," she said, coolly. I recognized the voice. It was Sandy. She was young, but wiser than her years and I liked her. We'd had a lot of fun together in that room and it had been the kind of fun that didn't leave me feeling sleazy in the morning. She was always open with me and expected nothing unreasonable.

Sandy was healthy and pretty and strong. If it had been anybody else at the door, I would have told them that I was asleep (unless it was Sophie, of course, but she was just a dream which was beginning to lose its definition and, besides, she didn't know where I lived). I let Sandy in. It was good to see her.

Tuesday was always the slowest night of the week. When I arrived at seven o'clock to relieve Soggy, the last happy hour customers were just reeling out of the bar. There was typically a lull period between the time when happy hour ended and when the night crowd showed up, so I had at least an hour to kill before I'd have to do anything even remotely resembling earning my nine dollar per hour wage. Soggy always left the bar clean and in perfect order, so all I could do was sit on a stool behind the bar and read a Stephen King book which he'd left behind.

At four pages into "The Stand," the door squeaked, announcing an arrival and I looked up to behold the glowing presence of Sophie. She was smiling. At me. The book in my hands vaporized as she glided across the room, alone.

"Hello Dave Mulligan," she said, with the same cheer and warmth in her words that had enchanted me a week earlier.

"Hi, Sophie," I probably said. Sophie then took the stool in front of me and got right to the point.

"I wasn't going to come back in here, but I wanted to thank you for the lovely note you wrote to me. No one's ever done anything like that for me before. I just had to let you know that I was quite touched by it, but there was no use in responding to it because I'm leaving New Zealand in less than a week."

"Where are you going?" I asked, sadly.

"Home to Belfast."

"Less than a week... does that mean six days?"

"Five, actually. My plane leaves Sunday at noon."

"Would you consider spending a little time with me before you leave?"

"I would... I really would, but what good would it do? Even if we were to get along in grand style, I have to go home."

"I understand that, but maybe we should look at this another way... we could become close friends in five days. We could create something positive where nothing existed before and then go our separate ways." I think we were both amazed at how soon we had gotten to this point in our conversation. It had developed so quickly that it was almost frightening, yet it was happening naturally and was completely unforced.

I felt, quite simply, as though we were "meant to be." I was going to say just that, when Sophie spoke again.

"I've been dying to know; what did you mean in your note when you said you didn't like yourself anymore? What's wrong with you?" She didn't have to ask twice. With that one question, she'd opened the gates and I told her everything; how I'd left home with the hopes of growing up, how I'd actually made some good progress and then how I'd had a serious relapse.

I had never been so honest with anybody in my life. I felt it was vital that she know everything about me before we proceeded any further. When I'd finished, I felt as though the great, dark shadow in which I'd been living had been lifted and I was worthy again to walk among the clean. I then thought to myself that if she didn't accept me, I deserved her rejection; and if she did accept me, she knew my whole story and there was nothing for me to hide.

"Do you think I'm a disgusting person?" I asked. She smiled.

"I think that some of the things you've done are rather shocking, but, no, I don't think you're disgusting. The fact that you think that what you've done is disgusting says to me that you're a decent man. I have to admit that I wouldn't envy your next girlfriend, but I'd certainly enjoy having you as my friend."

"So, you'll spend some time with me this week?"

"I'll be doing a lot of packing and sorting of my things..."

"Nobody packs and sorts for five days."

"I suppose I could find a little time here and there..."

"That's great! How about tomorrow?"

"What time tomorrow?" she asked.

"Well, I work at five... How about twelve? I'll buy you lunch and then we'll go out and see the sights of Christchurch together."

"That sounds very nice," she said, wearing a confident, comfortable, beautiful grin.

"You know something?" I said. "I was so concerned with telling you all about myself and confessing my sinful ways, that I still don't know anything about you."

"Well, my story pales in comparison to the Adventures of David. Are you sure you want to hear it?" she asked in her mild, perfect Irish accent.

"I'm sure." I was sure. I wanted nothing else. Sophie sipped a diet coke through a thin straw and told me her story.

She was a nurse. She'd been in New Zealand for a year. She'd followed her boyfriend there from Northern Ireland. He was a doctor. They'd lived together with several other doctors and nurses in a big house provided by the hospital. When she turned twenty-five, she could hear the ticking of her biological clock louder than ever, so she decided that it was time she and her man started thinking about beginning a family. But he wasn't ready. That old story (She was right, her story wasn't nearly as exciting as mine, but I was fascinated nonetheless).

She had given him an ultimatum, "Either make a baby with me, or I'll leave you and meet somebody who will." He stalled. She stood firm and held true to her threat and left. Well... left the room. She moved down the hall into a vacant bed and turned their relationship into a platonic one. She remained in the house because it was free and stayed on at the hospital.

She began to save money for her solo trip back to Northern Ireland. It had been three months since the break-up and Sophie claimed to be completely over him. I had my doubts about that, but I was just pleased to be with her.

When customers began to arrive and multiply, it became obvious that Sophie and I could no longer carry on our conversation with any degree of intimacy. She kept her seat at the bar, however and I topped off her diet coke and spoke with her whenever I could. She told me that she thought I was a very good barman and I told her that I had been looking for her all my life.

"I'm leaving in five days," she reminded me.

"We'll see about that," I said.

TWENTY

Sophie and Me

I arrived on the front steps of the Christchurch Art Museum at 11:30 the following morning, a half-hour early for my date with Sophie. I had woken up at eight, roughly three hours earlier than usual and rolled over with the intention of going back to sleep, but I was much too excited and gave up after flipping a dozen times on my squeaky bed. I got up and sat at my little desk to see if I could get anything done on my manuscript and managed to contrive one forced, awkward paragraph in an hour.

I then decided to see if writing a letter would come any easier and was pleased to find that it did. I wrote to my brother, whom I've always addressed as Brother, even in person. "Hello Brother, Like ninety percent of all letter-writers, I must first apologize for not writing for so long.

My excuse is rather pitiful, but it will serve to relieve both my guilt and some of your disappointment in my lack of correspondence. As you well know, I left on this adventure eight months ago with the hopes of "finding myself," of changing a few things about the way I am. My feeling all along, and the basis for my excuse, has been that if I were to stay in touch with you and everybody else back home, my changes would not be so apparent when I return at the end of my trip. I wanted this to be sort of a "before and after" kind of experiment. I've maintained in my mind an image of myself walking off the plane after disappearing for a year, with a few new lines around my eyes and a big, mountain-man beard. My voice would be deeper, my steps a little slower and I would be wiser. I would produce rustic, meaningful gifts from a sack made of burlap and share thought-provoking new philosophies.

It's become clear to me by now, though, that if I were to let my beard grow, it would look like one of those long, wispy ones that you see on very old Chinese men. And if my voice were to be any lower, it would only be due to too much drink and not enough sleep. Unfortunately, you see, all of the skeptics about my leaving on this trip were basically right; I've partied too much and slept with too many girls — just like I was doing back at home. I don't want to give you the wrong impression, I have had some wonderful adventures, but I've been irresponsible and have behaved like a kid whose parents have left for vacation. "When the cat's away, the mouse will play." Only this time, it's the mouse who's left town and he's having the time of his life. I still plan on salvaging something constructive out of this trip, though. I've got four months to go. I've got some stories to tell you when I get home.

Please spread the word that I'm okay. I'll see you at the airport in November; look for the mouse with the long, wispy beard. I love you, Brother. "Brother"

Christchurch was mostly cold and gray in July, but this particular day was sunny and crisp. It was just as cold as usual, but the brilliant blue sky helped warm my spirits and took the wet bite out of the air. I wore jeans and a sweater, and paced on the museum steps as I awaited Sophie's arrival.

At noon straight up, I saw her coming. She was a block away, walking very deliberately, with her hands in the pockets of her long, heavy coat and her head slightly down as if to improve her aerodynamics.

"You're a very animated walker," I said when she arrived. "I was going to walk toward you and meet you half way when I saw you coming, but then I would have robbed myself of the pleasure of witnessing your approach."

"Perhaps I was just eager to get here."

"To see me?"

"To see the museum," she said, smiling.

"Oh," I said, smiling back.

"Alright, and to see you, too. I admit it."

"Thanks," I said, feeling a wave of complete adoration wash over me, just as had happened the night we met.

"Would you mind terribly if we were to change our plans?" she said.

"I know we decided to meet here and go through the museum, but this is the loveliest day I've seen in months and it would be a shame to spend it indoors. I wonder if we might walk through the park instead? We could come back to the museum tomorrow, or another day perhaps."

"Sure. That's fine. It is a beautiful day... You scared me there for a second; I thought you were going to cancel our date."

"I wouldn't do that. I woke up extra early this morning to do my sorting and packing so that we could do this." The park in the center of Christchurch was huge, at least a couple of square miles. There were trails and paths going off in every direction. There were lakes and ponds, gardens and playing fields (In fact, I had played two rugby games on a field we passed together).

I was soon lost in the vast park, but my only concern in the world was Sophie. I recall wishing that the paths would go on and on forever so that we'd never have to end our walk on that perfect day in Christchurch.

We eventually came upon a small, glass-walled, octagonal restaurant called the Tea Kiosk in a clearing where many paths converged and we decided to have our lunch there. We ate sandwiches and drank pots of coffee and we made up long, detailed stories about any standout characters who passed by our window. Sophie's stories were invariably romantic...

"That handsome older gentleman there lost his wife ten years ago to an illness. He hasn't spoken a word since and he comes here each afternoon to feed bread to the ducks, because he and his wife used to do it here together."

"Do you think he'll ever re-marry?" I asked.

"Oh, no," she said adamantly, "never. He loved her far too much to ever let another woman into his heart."

My stories lacked Sophie's romance...

"I'm sure your story is very nice, but, I'm sorry, it's far from true. You see, that man is evil and has been married seven times. That isn't bread he's feeding to the ducks, but, small pieces of his seventh wife."

I realized something important as I sat there falling deeper and deeper in love with Sophie. Aside from the obvious enjoyment I derived from her company and the admiration I felt for her, I was struck by the fact that I was thoroughly enjoying being me. Quite simply, she made me feel affection for myself that I had not felt for a long time. I mentioned this to her and she said that it made her very happy and that I deserved my own affection.

As we left the restaurant and began our walk toward town, I turned to Sophie and asked,

"May I hold your hand?" She stopped and smiled at me and spoke as she slipped her small, soft, warm hand into mine.

"No one has ever asked me that before."

"I've wanted to all day, but everything has been going so well ... I was afraid I'd ruin it."

"I don't think it's ruined. Do you?" she asked, smiling and squeezing my hand slightly.

"No," I said. Sophie and I held hands the whole way back to the center of town. Dora, her English friend whom I'd met, was going to meet her at the Occidental at three o'clock and give her a lift home.

When Sophie and I arrived at the Oxy, it was only two-thirty. We sat down on the grass in the park across the street.

"Since we've a little extra time, why don't you show me where you live?" she asked.

I had told her about the boarding house, which was actually a Christchurch landmark due to the fact that it had been a home for wayward women for almost ninety years. She was familiar with it, but had never been inside. A visiting nurse friend of hers had stayed there and told Sophie that it was "rustic and charming," and Sophie had always been curious when she'd passed by it.

"Okay," I said, "but we'll have to hurry. It's a few blocks from here."

"I thought you said you were living in that old brick building that used to be a women's home," she said, looking confused.

"I am. I do live there..."

"Well," she said, pointing, "isn't that it right over there?"

I followed her finger to a large brick building on the other side of the park. Only half of the building was visible behind a large tree in the center of the park. It was about two hundred yards from where we sat. It did look a lot like it, but my boarding house was several blocks away.

"My place is a lot like that, but it's about a fifteen-minute walk from here." My eyes remained on the three storey brick affair on the other side of the park. There was something about the portion of the building visible to us which disturbed me. Something familiar. Then I spotted it.

There was an old pair of leather rugby boots on the ledge outside the second window from the right on the third floor. I had gotten into the habit of putting them there because they stunk up my room if I kept them inside. I was looking at my boarding house. I had been living there for ten weeks. And for ten weeks I had walked out of that very front door on my way to work, turned right and walked three blocks to Cathedral Square. When I arrived at the Square, I turned left and proceeded across it for approximately two hundred yards. I then turned left again on Colombo Street and walked three blocks to the Occidental.

I began to laugh out loud when the realization hit me, but quickly regained my composure because I didn't want Sophie to feel left out.

"I'm embarrassed to say this... you're not gonna believe it. That is where I live. For two and a half months it's taken me over ten minutes to get to work — if I hurried. If that big tree weren't there, I'd be able to see the Occidental from my window. I've done some really stupid things in my life, but nothing which even approaches this. I am, undoubtedly, the world's biggest asshole."

After making the 90 second walk from the Oxy to the boarding house, I brought Sophie upstairs to show her my room. I asked her to wait in the hall for a few moments so that I could "neaten up" the room a bit — this consisted, of course, of throwing all of my dirty clothes under my bed and into the armoire. I quickly made my bed also. When I let her in, she was very polite and acted as though it was the most charming little room she'd ever seen.

My mind had difficulty processing the fact that Sophie was actually standing in my room. I had unconsciously promoted her to celebrity status since I'd first set eyes on her and there she was, the incredible Sophie, standing next to my bed.

"If that mattress could only speak, I'm sure it would have some very interesting stories to tell," she said, catching me off-guard.

"I told you, those days are over."

"How can you be sure? I mean... how long has it been since your last conquest? Two weeks? A month?" I wasn't sure what to say. Sandy had spent the night with me only two nights before, but it had been a different kind of sexual encounter than the kinds about which I had described during the "great confession" I had made to Sophie when she'd come to visit me at the Oxy. I knew and liked Sandy. It was "good" sex, as opposed to "dirty" sex. I decided I couldn't lie to Sophie about it. If I were to lie, it would have tainted something perfect.

"Well, actually, it was pretty recent, but it wasn't a "conquest" ... it wasn't a one night stand. It was a girl that I've known for a while now. A girl that I like."

"I don't understand... if you're so fond of this girl, and you're sleeping with her, then why were you so intent upon seeing me?"

"I think I said that wrong... what I meant was, it wasn't like the kind of sex I told you about ... it was different, but I don't love her. I like her and I enjoy her company, that's all"

"I'll bet you do," she said. "How long has it been since you "enjoyed her company"? she asked, gesturing toward my bed with a backhand sweep of her arm.

"She was here the other night," I said, avoiding Sophie's eyes.

"The other night? Which other night?"

"She visited here Monday night."

"This Monday night? Two nights ago?"

"Yes."

"On the brink of me?" she asked, mouth wide open in disbelief.

"Yes. On the brink of you. I thought I'd never see you again." She shook her head.

"If you would have thought about it logically, Mulligan, the night we met was a Tuesday. In your note, you asked me to come back to the Occidental and meet you. I assumed that you'd expect me on the following Tuesday, so that's when I came."

"I never thought about it that way. I looked for you the whole next night and every night. When a week had gone by, I decided that you obviously weren't as taken by me as I was by you and that you weren't going to come back."

"Your patience is admirable. Six whole days. It must have been Hell for you." She shook her head again and punched me in the shoulder. While Sophie was certainly joking with me, there was a distant anger in her eyes and a crease in her brow which betrayed her joviality. This said to me that she was somewhat bothered by the fact that I had been with another girl since we'd met, though I accepted that it was probably more of a blow to her ego than it was to her heart.

"Believe me, Sophie, if I would have known that you were coming back — even though you're leaving in less than a week — I never would have done it. I meant everything I said in that note. If you were staying, I'd ask you to be my girlfriend, and I'd forget every other girl I've ever met."

"You'll forgive me when I scoff," she said. And then she scoffed.

"I think you should stay," I said, placing my hands on her shoulders. "I'm completely serious. I think you should call the airline and cancel your flight home. I realize that I deserve very little credibility when it comes to matters of romance, but you have to believe me. I fell in love with you that first night at the Occidental."

"If that were true, then you wouldn't have slept with that other girl."

"I can see why you would think that, but, like I said, I didn't think you were coming back."

"Alright," she said, knocking my hands off of her shoulders, "let's say that you really felt the way you say you felt. Even if you KNEW that you'd never see me again, you shouldn't have been able to be with another girl that soon."

"Hey," I said chuckling, "I had to get over you somehow." She punched me in the shoulder again. "You're a cad!" she charged.

"What's a cad?"

"A cad is a scoundrel. An ill-bred fellow."

"Now you're insulting my parents," I said, smiling.

"No, I'm not. They probably meant well, but you just turned out wrong."

"Will you cancel your flight?"

"Absolutely not."

"Will you postpone it for a week?"

"Not for a minute."

"May I kiss you before I walk you back to the Oxy?"

"I'd rather kiss a toad." I moved toward her and she backed slowly away from me, smiling slightly and maintaining a look of mock defiance.

"Ribbit," I said. "Ribbit. Ribbit." She continued to retreat until her back touched the wall. She had her hands up to keep me away. I moved forward until her hands were on my chest and then I pressed on. She pushed with light pressure and then surrendered. I slowly pressed my mouth to hers and she offered no reaction whatsoever. Nothing.

"You're a cad," she whispered against my lips. And then she began to kiss me back. I had two forces against me when I invited Sophie to stay the night with me after our wonderful, dream-like afternoon together. The first was Sophie's better judgement, which took me thirty minutes in my room, plus the length of our walk from my boarding house to the Oxy, to overcome. She finally agreed to stay with me only after I'd given my word that I wouldn't pressure her to "do anything good friends wouldn't do."

The second bastion of resistance stood in the squatty, immovable form of Dora, Sophie's best friend. Dora's own stormy romantic history had transformed her into a nightmare for a man in my position; Dora was the closest friend of the girl I loved and Dora was a man-hater. At forty-one, she wore her hair in a short, blunt "I hate men" cut. She'd recently gone through a bitter disengagement with her fourth husband.

Sophie told me the entire story. As the legal proceedings came to a close and the judge pronounced the divorce final, Dora crossed the court room and kicked her newest ex in the balls so hard he couldn't even scream. According to Sophie, Dora admitted to having launched similar vicious assaults against the balls of her three previous husbands as well.

The failure of this fourth and final attempt at marriage confirmed for Dora something which she'd always suspected; that she and men were simply not compatible. She became the Red Baron of feminists, a war-battered ace navigating the smoky skies of a man's world, seeking out dogfights and painting a new set of balls on her girthy fuselage with each new kill.

Just before Sophie and I entered the Occidental to meet with Dora, I stopped Sophie outside the door.

"I've changed my mind," I said.

"Changed your mind? About staying together tonight?"

"No. About telling Dora that we're staying together tonight. I don't think we should tell her."

"Why not? You're not afraid of Dora, are you?"

"Of course I'm not afraid of Dora."

"Then why shouldn't we tell her?"

"Because I'm terrified of Dora, that's why." Sophie put her arms around me and gave me a short kiss.

"We can wait until tomorrow to tell her if you prefer. Tonight we'll just play it up as though I'm going home. After she drops me off, I'll pack a bag and take a taxi back here while you're still working. We are going to have to tell her, though. I don't want to lie to her. She's the best friend I've got in New Zealand."

We entered the occidental hand-in-hand, but as we approached the swinging doors to Perry's, I stopped again. I could feel the powerful, man-hating force of Dora pulsating through the thin, wooden doors. I released Sophie's hand.

"Coward," she whispered. She then reclaimed my hand, and we pushed through the double doors together.

Dora was seated alone at a table in the middle of the room among many empty tables. It did not surprise me that she'd elected not to sit at the bar, because Soggy was on duty and Soggy was a man. She was reading a paperback (probably about a lesbian psycho killer), which she lowered when we entered. She looked at Sophie first and began to smile, but then zoomed in on our joined hands and winced. She then looked back at Sophie with an expression which said,

"Are you crazy? Do you know what you're doing?" Then Dora the Man Hater looked straight at my balls.

I was remarkably uncomfortable for the entire duration of our visit with Dora. She was not supportive of our relationship. She was not even neutral. She outlined several reasons why she felt that it was a mistake for us to see one another, one of which being that she questioned my intentions. Sophie, however, defended my honor and explained that we simply felt comfortable together and were going to get to know one another before Sophie left on Sunday. Dora didn't like it. Dora didn't like me. Dora, I could sense, was fighting urges to kick me.

After accompanying them out to Dora's car, I gave Sophie an uncomfortable kiss as Dora looked on.

"I'll see you tomorrow," I said to Sophie with a stealthy wink. Then I said good-bye to Dora.

"Do you have any idea what I'll do to you if you hurt this girl?" she asked, smiling in what I saw as a weak attempt to disguise the malice in her threat.

"I have a pretty good idea," I said. Andrew McInnes still crossed my mind at least once a day and I'd feel that familiar pang of guilt about not meeting him in Queenstown. I even harbored slim hopes of seeing him walking into Perry's some time. I'd told Sophie all about McInnes and shared with her some of our adventure stories. She thought they were hilarious and expressed her regrets about missing the opportunity to meet my legendary Adventure Brother.

I just happened to be thinking about how much McInnes would have loved Sophie as I stepped behind the bar to relieve Soggy and begin my shift at Perry's.

"G'day Master Dave."

"G'day Soggy." He stepped over to the phone on the end of the bar and pulled an envelope out from under it.

"Here y'are mate. This arrived for you today." He handed me the envelope. It was addressed:

"Kindly deliver to: Mr. David Mulligan Barman extraordinaire/ Adventure Brother/ Knight of Chivalry Occidental Hotel Christchurch" I laughed out loud and opened it.

"Dear Mulligan,

So sorry to have missed you on the Bungee Bridge in Queenstown. When the day and time of our planned rendezvous arrived and passed with no Mulligan in sight, I began to worry.

Can it be, I wondered, that young Mulligan has finally met his match in the form of some man, woman, mountain, or beast and is unable to conquer this obstacle without the aid of his faithful partner? Could he be trapped in the heart of some steamy, swampy jungle, up to his neck in quicksand, muttering through mud-caked lips "Adventure Brother... adventure brother..."?

Or, more realistically, might he be held up in a primitive mountain hospital, in the final throes of a rare and dreaded venereal disease which has left him without wit or penis? Poor Mulligan, I thought to myself, he was a valiant knight. No doubt, though, whatever the hurdle which prevented him from following his plan and making it to that bridge in Queenstown, no mortal man could have overcome it. On the third day of waiting I gave up hope. By that time, I'd come to know the men operating the bungee jumping business. After a jump, the customer would be lowered into a small manned rowboat in the middle of the river three hundred feet beneath the bridge and they'd be shuttled to the bank.

Over those three days, it had become quite apparent to me that these men on the bridge were not happy with the performance of the young man driving the boat. I overheard them several times saying that they felt that he was unreliable and even heard some whispering about his suspected drinking on the job.

As the day neared its end, one of the fellows was kind enough to offer me a jump free of charge. Well, being the adventurous type, as you may remember, and no longer feeling as though I should wait for Mulligan to indulge, I took him up on it and took the leap. What an absolute thrill! When I made it back up to the bridge some time later to thank them, they were preparing to leave. I described to them how exciting the jump had been for me and told them that if there was anything at all I didn't like about the entire experience, it was the poorly captained rowboat ride from the center of the river to the bank. I did insist, however, that the young man steering the boat was probably much better able to handle the craft when he hadn't been drinking quite so much.

Well, ten minutes later I had a job and the next morning I began rowing palpitating bungee jumpers to the river's edge for a hundred dollars a day.

The money was certainly difficult to walk away from, so I remained in Queenstown for five weeks. I managed to save an impressive sum before moving on to Auckland, where I am now. I've been here for a month and, while I'd love to provide you with more details of my stay and of my solo adventures, I'll be boarding an Air New Zealand jet bound for Bora Bora in approximately thirteen minutes.

You see, I'm seated in the airport lounge and I've just met a young Canadian lady to whom you served a cocktail in the Occidental Hotel less than two weeks ago. She described you as "amusingly self-assured" and claimed that you somehow managed to refer to both your penis and her breasts in a two-minute conversation.

Any doubt on my part as to whether or not it was you she was describing vanished. I hope you're still at the Occidental to receive this letter and I hope it finds you well. I'll attach my parents' address and phone number in Scotland (Troon). I can be reached through them at any time. I never really had a chance to convey to you what an honor it has been to be your Adventure Brother and fellow Knight of Chivalry.

I've never been as certain of anything as I am of the fact that our paths will cross again and there will be more adventures. For our next one, I'd like you to start considering parachuting into the Amazon. I must go now. Bora Bora beckons.

Andrew Cameron McInnes, Scotland

P.S ONWARD CREAMPUFF!!!"

Sophie made it back to the Occidental by ten-thirty, and she sat at the bar and read McInnes' letter as I cleaned up and prepared to close. It felt good to share him with her. She laughed and laughed as she read and said again how sorry she was to have missed out on meeting him and seeing us in action together. But I knew that he was right in what he'd said in the letter. We'd meet again.

I finished up and closed the bar by eleven. We first had a beer together and then swung by the Square and picked up a hot, heavy, greasy bag of fish 'n chips and walked hand-in-hand to the boarding house. It was nearly twelve o'clock when we arrived at the front door.

I don't know how many times I'd already made the same mistake; maybe twenty times. The front door was locked at eleven o'clock every night. There was a funny little built-in, push button combination lock on the front door. The building manager, a quiet old man whom the boarders had nick-named "Moses," changed the combination every three days and the new combination was written on a chalkboard on the wall around the corner in the vestibule ("The combination has been changed. The new combination is B-23. Please write it down. Don't wake me up if you forget it. I'm old and tired). I walked by this board every time I left the building but never remembered to look at it.

Moses had even attached a little pad and pen to make it easier to write oneself a note. The hour of my return varied, depending on how late I got off work, or whether or not I went out afterwards. Each time I came home and tried the lock and realized that the combination had been changed again, I would swear first and then try and think of an alternative to ringing the electric bell and waking poor, tired Moses.

The bell was designed to be used only by new customers in need of lodging. In fact, there was even a little sign beneath it saying just that. It rang only in the manager's apartment so that others wouldn't be awakened by late arrivals. On one occasion, I even tried climbing the fire escape to avoid bothering Moses, but ended up waking half the building when I accidently broke the window to an old, crazy woman's room and sent her into screaming fits. Several times when I'd resorted to ringing the bell, I'd had a different female with me when Moses finally appeared at the door. Visitors of this description were not formally forbidden, but were frowned upon by Moses. Literally.

He would open the door, frown at my guest, frown at me and shake his head as I apologized for getting him up again. I would have felt better if he would have gotten angry with me, but he only seemed to become more heavyhearted and even more tired. Sophie pointed out to me that I was merely prolonging the inevitable, so I finally rang the bell. It was several minutes before I saw Moses' worn slippers appear at the top of the stairs.

He looked just as unhappy as ever as he labored down the steps in his droopy pajamas and mussed white hair. I felt awful. When Sophie saw him, she put her hand to her mouth and said,

"Oh, the poor old dear, I think we woke him!" When Moses opened the door, Sophie took the lead and began to charm him before he'd even had a chance to frown or shake his head. She apologized without end and assured him that she would see to it that this would never happen again. Then she thanked him for allowing us in and gave him a big, warm hug. And for the first time ever, I saw a sparkle in the old man's eye.

"This is the girl you should keep," he said to me, smiling through a blush.

"This is the girl I love," I said.

Sophie and I sat on my squeaky old bed and ate our fish 'n chips straight out of the bag. There was so much to talk about. So much catching up to do. It was almost as though we were being reunited and there was an urgency to let each other know all that had happened during our separation.

Every few minutes I'd stop what I was saying, or I'd stop her in the middle of a sentence, to kiss her. I had no control over these urges. These kisses were soft, lingering expressions of my overwhelming, overflowing affection for her. I kissed her with my eyes open, for there was nothing I could imagine which could match the beauty of the vision before me.

I was startled when Sophie looked at her watch and announced that it was three a.m.. I was then struck by the sad realization that when the hour had passed midnight, it had become Thursday, meaning that I officially had one day fewer to spend with Sophie.

"That means that we've only got three days left."

"Let's not talk about that," she said, sadly.

"Isn't there any way you can postpone your flight?"

"No. I can't"

"Why not? If it's a money problem, I can certainly..."

"It's not that. It's my Mum. I haven't seen her for over a year. She'd be crushed if I didn't come. I did it to her once before. I told her I was coming home and then I decided to stay on and try to save some money. She'd planned a little party for me... and then I called her the night before I was supposed to come home. I could hear how excited she was when she answered the phone. And then I had to tell her that I wasn't coming. She cried and cried. She still cries every time I call. She's such a dear and so emotional, I just couldn't do that to her again. If it weren't for my Mum though, I'd stay with you."

This was certainly understandable, but discouraging nonetheless. I had allowed myself to believe over the last few hours that she may be changing her mind about leaving. As I flirted with Sophie, I'd also been flirting with the fantasy that she was slowly coming around. This was why I'd waited until after three in the morning to bring it up again. I was letting my fantasy develop. But now I had my answer. She was still going to leave and nothing was going to change that.

This made me feel almost insignificant in her life when I saw my petty crush on Sophie juxtaposed next to her love for her mother and her mother's love for her. Her reason was not something I could dispute. I couldn't say "Ah, c'mon, all moms cry. She'll be okay. Just stay for me."

When one dream burns, another is bound to sprout from its ashes. It's human nature to cultivate these fantasies in order to insulate ourselves from impending or passing disappointment. The next scenario I manufactured was one in which Sophie turned to me and said,

"I know! Why don't you come back to Northern Ireland with me? I'd like you to meet my parents!" This one I didn't dare verbalize because I didn't want to risk its early demise. If I were to reveal it, and she didn't embrace it with equal enthusiasm, it would not only mean an awkward moment of complete humiliation, it would also spell out in bold letters that there was no hope for Sophie and me.

At 5am Sophie said she'd like to wash up and put on her pajamas. She picked up her overnight bag and I directed her to the bathroom across the hall from my room. I then sat back on my bed alone. Well, not quite alone...

"So... ya gonna slip her the ol' pork sausage?"

"Of course not! Go away, you don't belong here."

"What do you think she meant by 'pajamas'? Maybe one of those teddys?"

"I don't know. Just pajamas. They're probably flannel."

"Flannel? Only married women and battle-axes wear flannel. Maybe in Northern Ireland when they say 'pajamas' they mean panties. Maybe she's going to come back in here wearing little, tiny, see-through panties. Get ready. Get naked."

"That's enough! I don't want you here. I love Sophie. She's not like any of the other girls. She's too good for you to be here."

"Who are you kidding? She's too good for either one of us." I heard light footsteps patter across the hall and then the door slowly opened with a squeak. Sophie left the shadow of the hall and entered the dim light of my room. I paused at least a second before looking at her, for I knew that she was still a little nervous about being there and I didn't want to validate her apprehension by appearing to be over-eager to see her in her pajamas.

When I turned I saw that she was wearing beautiful, elegant, light green silk pajamas; the same smoky green as her eyes. They were loose-fitting, yet quite revealing where the silk lay against her skin and I couldn't help but behold the incontrovertible, and most un-ignorable, presence of a magnificent pair of melon-sized breasts. Every time I'd seen Sophie, she'd been wearing a big sweater or a coat or something else which concealed the nature of her curves.

But now she stood before me with only a veil of silk between her body and the rest of the universe. I was just about to utter something about how nice she looked when I realized that the little voice had not yet left the room and he spoke before I had a chance to stop him.

"Damn. I never realized you had such big McGuffys." The McGuffy incident was the only blemish on a long, otherwise perfect, day. Sophie forgave me after considering several minutes of sincere apology and even laughed about my callous comment upon regaining her composure. I wasn't completely certain that everything was going to be okay, though, until Sophie punched me in the arm. Then I knew that I was forgiven.

When the potentially awkward moment arrived and it was time to crawl under the covers, I did my best to set Sophie's mind at ease. I asked her to sit beside me on the edge of the bed. Then I took her hand in mine and looked into her eyes.

"Your trust means everything to me. I want you to feel comfortable sleeping here with me. I meant it when I said that I wouldn't put you in an awkward position. I'm just going to enjoy holding you and having you here with me. There isn't another place in the entire world that I'd rather be; there isn't another moment in my past that I'd rather revisit. Right here, right now is where my dreams have taken me, and you'll be safe in my arms." The term "bittersweet" never applied to anything as well as it did to my next three days with the wonderful Sophie.

Sophie and I walked and played and ate and drank and laughed all day, each day, and ended up in my little room. And no matter how wonderful the day had been, this was always our favorite part, when we'd share a big bag of fish 'n chips from the little shop in the square in the middle of the night on my squeaky, old bed. We were too alive to sleep.

Yet, even at these highest peaks of our new-found love, it was impossible to ignore the dark cloud of Sophie's impending departure looming on the horizon. Sophie and I clung to the final moments of our last night together, yet, despite our efforts, Saturday night slipped away, and our last day had begun.

At four a.m., we slid under the blankets to snuggle and hold each other for the last time. My desire to make love to Sophie was almost overwhelming. Actually, that sounds a bit misleading, because it implies that just one or two more degrees of desire on my part would have put me over the top and I would have expressed to her my carnal longing. But nothing could have made me do so.

As intense as my craving for her was, I had given her my word that I wouldn't make her uncomfortable by making a pass at her, and keeping my word had become even more important to me than the prospect of having sex with her. Apparently, however, I'd been groaning involuntarily as we kissed.

"Are you going to be alright?," she asked, arousing me from a good hormone trance.

"Yeah, I'm okay, why?"

"Because you were making odd sounds."

"I'm sorry. I didn't know I was."

"You sounded as though you're tortured."

"'Tortured'? I'm about as far from tortured as I could be. I'm having the best time of my life."

"Mull?" (She liked calling me Mull).

"Yes?"

"Would you like to make love with me, Mull?" Well, if my head were on a swivel, it would have spun so fast it would have hummed.

Hearing Sophie ask me that was the very last thing I expected. This was a girl who had been intimate with only two men in all of her twenty-five years. Where she was raised, it just wasn't done outside of marriage. And there she was, in my bed, offering herself to me.

"I don't think so," I said.

"What?" she asked, baffled.

"No," I said.

"No?" She was shocked. So was I.

"Well," I continued, "you know I want to. That's obvious. But I'm not going to."

"Why not?"

"Because I want to show you that that's not why I'm here with you."

"I know that now. It's okay. I want to make love with you."

"No."

"Mull..."

"I'm sorry. I don't want this relationship to end when you leave tomorrow ... or today, actually, your plane leaves in eight hours. I don't want you to get home to Belfast and think, 'Why did I do that? That damn Mulligan was just like I thought he was, and he got just what he wanted from me'. So, I'm not going to make love to you."

"Please Mull?"

"Sorry. No."

"Don't you say sorry to me, you bastard!" she suddenly blurted out, snarling. She then punched me in the shoulder.

"You just love this, don't you? There you were, mister bloody Casanova when I met you, sleeping with every tart in Christchurch, even one on the Brink of Me, and now here you're rejecting me in your bed. You're having fun, aren't you Mull?" Her accent was much stronger when she was ruffled.

"I love you," I said, smiling. I then moved to kiss her. She quickly turned her head and my lips found her cheek.

"Well, you've a bloody strange way of showin' it," she said.

"Do you love me?" I asked.

"I might."

"Do you?"

"Yes."

"Then say it."

"Okay. I love you. Now take off your knickers and make love to me because you'll not be gettin' another chance!"

"That's not true. We'll make love the next time we see each other."

"But we've no idea how long that's going to be."

"Maybe it won't be very long at all. We could both start saving money as soon as we get home and pitch in together and one of us will fly to see the other."

"That'll be fine, sure, but it may take months, and it doesn't do me any good right now, does it Mull?"

"We'll make love when we see each other again. It'll make it that much better"

"You're a bastard."

"I love you."

"I love you too, you bastard. I'm sad to be leaving you"

"I'm sad too." We held each other and waited for sleep.

At ten-fifteen a.m. Sophie and I were startled from our sleep by a violent pounding on my door. It was Dora. We had over-slept. Sophie was supposed to have met Dora in front of the boarding house at ten for a ride to the airport. Her luggage was all packed and ready to go in the back of Dora's car. Everything was prepared, except for Sophie. She rushed across the hall in a panic and got in the shower.

It was the worst kind of good-bye. We had planned on being up by nine so that we could have coffee together, but our lack of sleep had caught up with us and we'd slept right through.

Sophie had made the decision up front that I would not accompany her and Dora to the airport. She felt that it would be less painful if we said our farewells there at the boarding house. This left me approximately three minutes to say good-bye to her. Dora showed some uncharacteristic sensitivity and waited in the hall. I put my arms around Sophie and held her tightly,

"Dammit," I said. "I wish we had more time. This is happening too fast."

"I'm sorry, Mull."

"It's not your fault. I had an amazing time with you, Sophie. You're the most wonderful girl I've ever met. I'd do anything to keep you, but I guess it's just not meant to be right now." She took out a tissue.

"Isn't it incredible, Mull, that you came all the way from America, and I came all the way from Northern Ireland, and we met in New Zealand? Think of it. When we were kids growing up, what were the odds of our ever meeting? Isn't it a wonderful world, Mull?"

"You sure make it seem that way. You've changed me, you know."

"I didn't change you. You grew tired of being the way you were, and I just happened to be with you when it happened."

"No. I did it for you, Sophie."

"Well, you'd better not change back then after I leave. If I hear about you getting back together with the "Brink" or any of those other bimbos again, I'll come back and box your ears."

"I promise I won't. I'll be leaving soon anyway. I don't want to be here anymore." This was true. Suddenly I couldn't stand the thought of remaining in Christchurch without Sophie.

"So, you'll be going to the islands then?"

"Yeah. Rarotonga first. Then Fiji." Even the blind and reckless expedition onto which I was about to embark into the South Pacific Islands had lost much of its shimmer. The prospect of life after Sophie seemed almost dreary, like when Dorothy returns to a grey, colorless Kansas following her adventures in the explosively colorful Oz. "I have no idea what to expect in those places," I said. "But I do know that there's nothing in the world I'd love more than to experience them with you. Just imagine the adventures we could have!"

During a moment of complete desperation and hopelessness such as this one, it is a natural defense mechanism for a man to express his greatest dreams of what may have been. It's a last grasp, and it provides a few moments of happiness and a hollow smile.

"I know, Mull. It would have been incredible."

"I love you, Sophie."

"I love you too, Mull." The timing of Dora's knock at the door indicated that she'd probably been listening. "It's time to go Sophie. You don't want to miss your plane."

"Oh, I have to go. Please write me every day, and think about me when you're on the beach in Rarotonga."

"You're damn right I'll be thinking about you. I never got to see you in a bikini."

"You mean you never got to see my McGuffys in a bikini."

"Yes." We laughed together and shared sad smiles and happy tears.

"Good-bye, Mull."

"Good-bye, Sophie."

We kissed once more, and she was gone.

TWENTY-ONE

Until We Meet Again

My first impulse was to curl up on my bed and sulk about Sophie, but this didn't last long. It was overpowered and replaced by my desire to leave Christchurch, so I sprung out of bed, cleaned up my act, and headed downstairs to give my notice to Moses.

"What about Sophie?" he asked. He was very fond of Sophie.

"She left. So, I am too."

"You let her go?"

"I had no choice."

"There's always a choice, mate. You just didn't try hard enough." This hit home and made me wonder. Had I not tried hard enough? Had I not been convincing enough when expressing my love? Or maybe it just boiled down to the fact that she simply was not as fond of me as I was of her. I hadn't really thought of Sophie's leaving as a personal failure until that moment.

"I tried everything," I said to Moses.

"Did you ask her to marry you?"

"No, it was a little early for that. I only met her about ten days ago."

"Well," he said, "then don't tell me you tried everything."

"Everything within reason," I replied.

"Even after ten days, if it's right, it's right, and anything is within reason. Truthfully, mate. I'm an old man. I used to be a lot like you. I don't even want to guess how many thousands of girls I've met. But that Sophie of yours was special. She'd be worth chasing, and you're still young enough to do it."

My next stop was the Oxy to let them know that I'd be leaving. I'd give Diane as long a notice as she wanted me to because she'd been a good boss to me and had been patient with me when I met Sophie and had allowed me to cover my shifts so that I could spend those final days with her. She told me that she was sorry to hear that I'd be leaving and that I could take off as soon as I liked because there were currently more than enough bartenders willing to take my shifts.

She then told Soggy to buy me a drink, and I sat at the bar in Perry's and considered getting drunk. This was a time for introspection. Personal inventory. I'd meant what I said to Sophie about her changing me. I did feel different. Improved. Cleansed.

I thought about what Moses had said to me about chasing her. She was worth it, certainly. I had enough money saved to buy myself a ticket to Northern Ireland, but what would I do when I got there? Tend bar again under the table? It would be fun to work in an old Irish pub, but it didn't represent the most promising of futures. I decided that it would be best for me to head back to the States, via the Islands, and get a real job. That seemed to me the most realistic and responsible way to earn a position at Sophie's side.

Suddenly, I was almost shocked by how much I sounded like my father. What I had decided was exactly what he would have suggested I do. Was I growing up? Was I doing it for myself, or was I doing it for Sophie? Did it matter? My final decision was that I would leave New Zealand as soon as possible, spend maybe a week in the tropical islands of the South Pacific, and head back home to organize my life.

Much of this I shared with my friend Soggy across the bar. He agreed with me that Sophie was well worth chasing. He, too, had grown quite fond of her in that short period when she'd graced the Occidental with her presence.

He also agreed with my strategy of going home first in order to get her back in the long run. "Delayed gratification" was the term he used, and, again, I thought of my father. At noon straight up, the exact moment when Sophie's plane was leaving New Zealand soil, I raised my DB and gazed skyward.

"Here's to Sophie. Until we meet again." Two DB's later I was pondering leaving Perry's and heading over to the corner travel agency to arrange my flight to Rarotonga. I mentioned this to Soggy, and he said,

"Rarotonga?" He envisioned a bamboo runway and hordes of natives fleeing in terror from the giant bird as it swooped from the clouds.

"Then, of course," I added, "I'd emerge from the plane, holding a cold beer, and they'd make me a god."

"And what would your first official act be as god of Rarotonga?" he asked. "No, let me guess. You'd outlaw clothing entirely and encourage daily virginal sacrifices."

"No. My first official act as God of Rarotonga would be to appoint my own Goddess. And the first goddess of Rarotonga would speak with an Irish accent." I thanked Soggy for the beers and told him that I was off to make a plane reservation. He suddenly wore a strange expression, and I was about to ask him what he was thinking when he said "Don't look now, but there's a goddess standing right behind you." I spun on my stool, and I was facing Sophie. A second later I held her tightly in my arms. I was overwhelmed with joy.

"Are you really here?" I asked with tears in my eyes.

"Yes. I'm here." I could see then that she'd been crying.

"What's wrong? Did you miss your plane?"

"No," she said, sniffling, "I didn't miss it. I was all checked in, sitting in the boarding area. A lovely old lady next to me asked why I seemed so upset, and I told her about you. She told me a story about a boy named James she'd met fifty years ago when she spent a summer visiting her grandmother in England. They fell in love, but when the summer ended, she had to go back home. He told her that he'd follow her as soon as he could afford it. He worked two jobs for six months and saved enough for a ticket on a ship. That was just at the beginning of the war, though, and the Germans sank the ship he was on, and he was lost. She was devastated when she heard the news. A month later she received a poem that he'd mailed to her the day before his ship left England. It said: 'I'd give all the days from Then through Forever, for the cherished few moments when we are together'

"Isn't that beautiful?" Sophie asked, wiping her tears with a wadded tissue.

"The dear old woman said that she still thinks about James almost every day, and it's been over fifty years. I don't know what's going to happen with us, Mull, but I'd hate to make a decision now that I'll regret for the rest of my life." I held Sophie tightly against me as she cried on my shoulder.

"It's been a hard day for me, Mull. First, I had to say goodbye to you, then I heard that sad story, and then, I had to call my mum. I told her the story about James, and that I loved you, and that I was scared I might never see you again if I left. She cried and told me to stay with you."

"I love your mother," I said.

"Will you please take me back to your room?" she asked me, quietly. I carried Sophie's luggage and we walked side by side across the park toward my little room.

EPILOGUE

A Crowded Sky

I was a little concerned about Sophie seeing me with flight face, but I figured that she'd have it too, so what the hell? She'd fallen asleep anyway about an hour into the flight, wasting a good window seat and leaving me alone.

At first, she'd slept prettily, but as she sank deeper into complete slumber, her mouth hung open and she began to snore. She looked adorable, so I took out the camera we'd purchased together and snapped a close-up. The flash startled her, but not enough to bring her out of it. She puckered her eyes, clamped her mouth shut, and turned toward the window.

A minute later her mouth hung open again. Since my only reason to stay awake was asleep next to me, I took the last swallow of my warm Steinlager and reclined my seat the full, unsatisfying three inches which Mr. Boeing had been kind enough to allow me. Over Sophie's head, I could see that the sun was melting into the sea. I drifted off into the purple-orange glow and met my maker.

He was looking out over the sea. A glass of red wine rested between his hands on the wooden railing in front of him. He shook his head slowly in awe of yet another incredible, Southern California sunset. I watched him in silence. I was always amused by the amount of pleasure he derived from that view.

"I've never even heard of Rarotonga," he said. "Sounds like a place invented for an Abbot and Costello movie. I can see Lou sniveling in a giant kettle of water, surrounded by spear-toting natives."

"I'd never heard of it either. I still don't know anything about it. It'll be an adventure."

"Another adventure? You've got adventures coming out of your ass. Aren't you tired of them yet?"

"Well, this will be the last one for a while..."

"And then what? When does the adventure end, and the rest of your life begin?"

"It already has begun. You see, I've recently discovered, dad, that 'adventure' and 'real life' don't have to be mutually exclusive. I've got Sophie with me now, and she makes it all real.

"And what do you propose to do to keep her?"

"Well, I haven't decided exactly what I'm going to do when I get home. But I do know that there'll be no more fucking around. I figure I can't be an asshole and expect somebody like Sophie to stick around. I'm lucky to have her."

"She's lucky to have you, too, son."

"You know something, dad? I think you'd still love me no matter what I did. I think you love me unconditionally, and that says more about you as a father than it does about me as a son. And maybe that's been my problem all along. I knew that no matter what I did — or didn't do - you'd still love me. I took it for granted and it ended up back-firing on me. I sometimes feel that I was a disappointment to you and there's no way I can change that."

"You're wrong. I may have been disappointed about a few instances when you failed to complete something you started, like college, but I was never disappointed in you as a man. I was always proud of who you are and I knew all along that you'd end up doing well. I just became a little impatient with you at times, that's all. It was like watching a Porsche driving around in first gear."

"Well, I think I'm ready to shift now."

"I think you already have."

"I love you, Dad."

"I love you too, Son. But you already know that. It's unconditional." When I awoke, I saw that Sophie was still asleep, still open-mouthed and facing the window, which was now black.

I then began to imagine what Rarotonga would be like. We'd purposely not found out any details about the island because we wanted it to be a complete surprise. We had no idea of how big it was, how many people were there, or even where we were going to stay.

All we knew was that it was one of the Cook Islands and that it had an airport capable of handling a hundred-passenger jet. I sat on the aisle and imagined turquoise waters, lapping at beautiful, white sand beaches, lined with palms swaying gently in the warm breeze...

"Yeah, and here and there a big-titted native girl lying in the sand. I bet they're all beautiful. I think I heard once that they're almost always naked, and that if you just shake a man's hand and give him a Bic lighter, you can have his daughter for the weekend. Wouldn't that be great, Dave? Dave? Dave! I know you can hear me..."

THE END

about the author

Dave Mulligan is a married father of three, living on the Truckee River in Reno, Nevada.

He hosts and produces a family travel series called Great Getaways and still enjoys creating new adventures and seeing the world. He'll always miss his father, dearly, and is currently working on his next book.

CPSIA information can be obtained
at www.ICGtesting.com
Printed in the USA
BVOW09s1530070218
507479BV00001B/77/P